THE INDISPENSABLE YOUTH PASTOR

LAND, LOVE, AND LOCK IN YOUR YOUTH MINISTRY DREAM JOB

MARK DEVRIES & JEFF DUNN-RANKIN

The Indispensable Youth Pastor
Land, Love, and Lock In Your Youth Ministry Dream Job

Credits
Authors: Mark DeVries and Jeff Dunn-Rankin
Executive Developer: Nadim Najm
Chief Creative Officer: Joani Schultz
Copy Editor: Rob Cunningham
Cover Art and Production: Natalie Johnson and Riley Hall
Production Manager: DeAnne Lear

ISBN 978-0-7644-6610-6

10 9 8 7 6 5 4 3 2 1   20 19 18 17 16 15 14 13 12 11

Printed in the United States of America.

DEDICATION

To Dad, for wisdom and opportunity.

To Mom, for vision and faith.

—Jeff

To Parish and Nealie, may the churches you
grow up in help you love Jesus more because
of what your Abu does.

—Mark

CONTENTS

SECTION TWO | HOW TO LOCK IN YOUR YOUTH MINISTRY DREAM JOB

SECTION THREE | HOW TO LOVE YOUR YOUTH MINISTRY JOB

THEY CALL IT WORK FOR A REASON

A year or so ago, I had the privilege of doing a phone interview with a group of youth ministry majors in Duffy Robbins' senior seminar at Eastern University. In characteristic Duffy style, he started the interview tongue in cheek and asked:

"Uh…Mark…My class liked your book and everything. But after reading *Sustainable Youth Ministry*, a number of my youth ministry majors are beginning to wonder if God's will for their lives might have changed. How do you feel about writing a book that makes people less excited about doing youth ministry?"

I laughed and said, "I'm actually thrilled!"

"Sorry?"

I answered, giving this class the very same message I knew they had heard in every youth ministry class they had taken at Eastern:

"In my work as a consultant, I get to see way too many fried youth workers. These are folks who were expecting their jobs to be a whole lot like being camp counselors. Then they find themselves overwhelmed, facing a dizzying combination of expectations they are totally unprepared for.

"Sadly, I get to see people on the other side—people who entered the world of youth ministry bright-eyed and passionate but leave prematurely, burned out and skulking away from ministry and often from the church altogether.

"The real tragedy," I explained, "is that *it doesn't have to be this way.*

"The time to decide about a 'call' to youth ministry is not *after* you get hired by a church, fall in love with a group of kids, and find the pieces of the ministry falling apart all around you. The time to make that decision is now.

"So, I'm *thrilled*—thrilled for this group of soon-to-be youth workers to have their eyes wide-open to what they are stepping into."

I imagine the students on the other end of the conference call with hands in the air, joking with their professor, "*Now* you tell me! Thanks a lot!"

LANDING, LOVING, AND LOCKING IN

For almost a decade now, we've been privileged to work with hundreds of youth workers, helping them find the right fit, build sustainable youth ministries, and set up systems that allow them to love their work more with each passing year. And through lots of encounters with people just like you, we've stumbled onto a few principles that have the power to transform the way you approach your next (or your current) call in youth ministry.

Here's what we've observed: There are people who can *land* a youth ministry job but soon find themselves detesting the job they've gotten. There are others who have everything it takes to build a sustainable youth ministry but just can't seem to get their foot in the door. And there are still others who love their ministries but work with the any-day-now threat of losing their jobs for reasons that feel mysterious and unknowable.

The dance of having a vocation in youth ministry requires all three skills: landing, loving, and locking in your dream youth ministry job. And this book is written to equip you for all three.

Because of our short attention spans (and yours), we've divided this book into short chapters. The stories we tell are true, although we often change the names, locations, and details to protect the innocent and guilty alike. And every now and then we've taken the liberty of creating parables to illustrate a principle or two.

Jeff and I have had the privilege of working side by side for many of the last 25 years. And most recently, we've been honored to lead the Youth Ministry Architects team together. Both of us still serve on staff at our churches, leading their youth ministries. And both of us imagine ourselves working as youth pastors until our families check us into our respective nursing homes.

As you might imagine, when two old friends tell stories about their shared experiences, the details of who did what can get confusing. So for the sake of simplicity, we decided to write this book in one voice. Here's how that will play out in the pages you're about to read:

When we speak of "we," we're talking about Jeff and me.

When you read "I" or "me" in a personal anecdote (like the Duffy story or the sentence above), it's Mark talking. Though the stories may be in my voice, these are our stories, not just mine.

When you see the name Jeff at any point in the book, it's not a random youth worker named Jeff; it is my co-author, Jeff Dunn-Rankin.

Ready?

A friend of ours once told us, "When you are prepared to do whatever it takes, you almost never have to do whatever it takes." He was talking about building a healthy marriage, but the same can be said for those who want to build a thriving youth ministry.

One of the most fascinating paradoxes of youth ministry is this: Those who are prepared for how hard youth ministry is, often and mysteriously, are those who discover it's not that hard after all.

In many ways, our little book here is simply a footnote to Jesus' words:

> "BUT DON'T BEGIN UNTIL YOU COUNT THE COST. FOR WHO WOULD BEGIN CONSTRUCTION OF A BUILDING WITHOUT FIRST CALCULATING THE COST TO SEE IF THERE IS ENOUGH MONEY TO FINISH IT?" (LUKE 14:28).

Every youth ministry is costly—exhausting, overwhelming, captivating, tedious, energizing, demanding, draining, and, at times, severely stressful. To enter into this vocation without eyes wide-open to those challenges virtually guarantees being blindsided and overwhelmed by the very situations that a well-prepared youth worker will handle with ease.

In his book *Youth Ministry From the Inside Out*, Mike Higgs paints a haunting picture of the littered landscape of youth ministry: "Sadly, the longer you are in youth ministry, the longer the list of sidelined and flatlined comrades becomes. And the obvious question is *why?*"

In the pages that follow, we'll answer the "why" question; but more importantly, we'll be answering the "how" question, providing the tools you'll need to stay in the game of youth ministry for as long as God has called you.

Prepare to be prepared.

HOW TO LAND THE YOUTH MINISTRY JOB YOU'LL LOVE

SECTION ONE

You may have started reading in this section because you are in search of your next, maybe your first, youth ministry position. Maybe you're just a compliant reader, and you're here because it's the next page in the book.

If you are happy in your current role and not even considering a search, you'll probably want to skip most of this section and save it for later. *But before you do...*

Make sure you read Chapters 1-4. These pages apply to everyone in youth ministry and will serve as a foundation for all that we have to say in Sections Two and Three.

FIRST THINGS FIRST

CHAPTER 1

("I AM THE VINE; YOU ARE THE
BRANCHES...APART FROM ME YOU CAN
DO NOTHING" (JOHN 15:5).)

Jeff (my co-author) had been a youth ministry volunteer for more than 15 years when God began to nudge him toward full-time ministry at his local church. He resisted mightily, with a long list of reasons why it would just be plain silly for him to leave his job as a newspaper editor.

As he rehearsed his list of excuses to his wife, he came up with a new one: "...and besides, I don't even read the Bible myself! How can I teach my youth to do what I don't do?!"

Mary Lou looked at him sweetly and said, "Don't you think you need to be doing that anyway—whether you become a youth pastor or not?"

Jeff hated the sting. But he knew Mary Lou was right (again).

Jeff responded to Mary Lou's challenge by starting reading. And it was in his process of reading through Ecclesiastes (of all books!) that he began to wake up to the possibility that God really might be calling him into full-time youth ministry. It was during this season that he landed in his first youth ministry job, at the church he already attended. And more than a decade later, he's still there.

MINISTRY OUT OF WHO WE ARE

Edwin Friedman in *A Failure of Nerve* said the same thing: "Children rarely succeed in rising above the maturity level of their parent, and this principle applies to all mentoring, healing, or administrative relationships."[1]

We might be able to fake our way through the job interviews, but we just can't fake our way through a ministry with teenagers for very long.

The only way to *share* a vibrant faith is to *have* a vibrant faith. And as sure as an acorn becomes an oak, we can only reproduce what we are.

In his book *What I Wish My Youth Leader Knew About Youth Ministry*, Mike Nappa reported that among the teenagers he surveyed, the quality they were looking for *most* in a youth leader was someone who was following and loving Jesus Christ themselves. More than a "cool" youth pastor or tech-savvy youth pastor, more than a great teacher or someone who can lead entertaining programs, teenagers reported that they *first* wanted leaders who were actually living out their faith themselves.[2]

It's not that there aren't dry seasons. There's no single "right" formula for staying anchored in our own faith. The key is to do something to grow in our own faith (even if that "something" is deliberately doing "nothing" in silence before God). Our students don't need to see perfection. What they do need to see is our purposeful, genuine, even stumbling pursuit of God for ourselves.

Of course, as disciples of Jesus Christ, we pursue God for God's own sake. But when we pursue God intentionally, it will undeniably impact our ministries and our search for the right ministry in three specific ways:

Call and discernment. The search for a position in youth ministry is no normal job search. Nowhere does the literal meaning of the word "vocation" hold more true than in the vocation of ministry. The word vocation, of course, shares the same root as the word "voice." And time for listening to God will be key to hearing the voice of our peculiar calling.

3

Bread for the long journey. Whether you're searching for a youth ministry position or have landed one, you'll need to stay healthy during the long journey. When no one is responding to your e-mails or when the third church has passed on your résumé, you need something more than a pat on the back and a stiff upper lip. Or when potential volunteers don't respond to your phone calls or when your attempts at starting new programs fall flat (again), being anchored in Christ has a way of keeping you walking when you feel like quitting.

Transparency. Though they may not be able to tell immediately, teenagers can often see through the veil of our own superficial faith—and so can a good search committee. Part of the reason for an on-site interview is to give the church a chance to get a sense of who we are beyond a résumé. Often, when churches describe the people they have hired, we hear hard-to-define phrases like "authentic faith" and "anchored." Churches are looking for those who not only can "do the work" but also those who exhibit the Fruit of the Spirit: love, joy, peace—all the way down to self-control. And fruit only grows when it is cultivated.

When we asked Pastor José to describe his youth director's greatest assets, he said, "I love the way he lives his life, the way he treats his family, and the way he demonstrates faith just by 'doing life' in full view of the youth group kids."

So take the tip from the flight attendant: "Please make sure your own oxygen mask is secure before attempting to help others."

We just can't share what we just don't have.

IF YOU WANT TO DO YOUTH MINISTRY, WE SUGGEST YOU...

CHAPTER 2

The auditorium was filled with writers—OK, would-be writers.

After four arduous years studying to write, the graduating class was thrilled to hear the wisdom of one of the most successful writers ever to walk the planet.

For reasons known only to him, this famous author had said an unexpected yes to the invitation to speak at commencement. And so, this group of eager young graduates, each dreaming of a career as a writer, sat poised to glean some insider secrets about actually making it in a field where so few actually do.

But what they heard stunned everyone in the crowded hall.

The speaker started out with a fine, if unoriginal, listener-getting device: "How many of you want to be writers?" Almost every graduate raised a hand—some eager and confident, others timid and doubting.

After the hands were lowered, the speaker paused. An uncomfortably long pause.

He began again, "If you hope to be writers, then…I suggest you write." He gazed into the eyes of his captive audience—and sat down.

We've met many young men and women who say they *really, really, really* want to do youth ministry, but they are not actually doing it—some have never done it. They are quick to explain that they just don't have time or they just can't find the right church or they are ready to serve but no one has asked them.

But working in an imperfect church, juggling an overloaded schedule, and taking initiative despite what other people do will be part and parcel of any job in youth ministry. If you are not currently serving in a youth ministry, do not pass go, do not perfect your résumé, do not even start applying yet. Find a youth ministry where you can serve first. If you want to land a satisfying job in the world of youth ministry, first learn what it feels like to be a volunteer and work to become the MVP on your church's volunteer ministry team.

When we see a résumé of someone who is applying for a youth ministry job but who isn't doing youth ministry, we know what that person wants.

They want a job.

But youth ministry, as a job, is challenging, often overwhelming, and the paycheck is seldom enough to keep us in the game. As a volunteer, you may discover how much you love this work, or you may actually realize this is not a calling you want to pursue. It just makes sense that you make this discovery before you (and the church) go to all the trouble of getting you hired.

Searching churches will look for one quality more than any other: proven results. So if you don't have any youth ministry results you can point to, get some. Plan a retreat, oversee volunteer recruitment, or make it your goal to increase the involvement of students in your ministry by 10 percent in the next six months. These will be the kinds of results that will catch the attention of searching churches.

If you think God may have a call on your life to serve in youth ministry, by all means, pursue it. But take the time to let your heart burn deeply to see teenagers—real, breathing, sometimes annoying teenagers—walk more deeply with Christ. Take the time to experience the heartbreak of praying and praying for specific students and seeing no visible fruit.

You and those touched by your future ministry will be grateful that you did. To paraphrase: If you want to do youth ministry, then *do* youth ministry…starting now.

THE MOST IMPORTANT YOUTH MINISTRY SKILL *EVER*

CHAPTER 3

Before we get starting talking about how to *land* your next job in youth ministry, there is someone we'd like you to meet.

This person will, without a doubt, be the most important asset you will *ever* have on a youth ministry team—a committed follower of Jesus, someone who loves kids and has strong gifts for ministry. This is someone with the *exact* gifts you will need not only to get the youth ministry job of your dreams but also to move that ministry from where it is to where you want it to be.

But before we make the introduction, we need to warn you. This person has a problem. Several, actually.

The biggest problem is that this person actually doesn't *know* about the problem. And to make things more personal, this character has the power to cripple *your* future ministry one day.

Though this person *could* become aware of his or her problems and actually do something about them, there remain areas where this person chooses to stay in the dark, steadfastly refusing to grow, clinging to unhelpful habits and behaviors.

Because this one individual has such pivotal power in setting the trajectory of your ministry, you'll want to get a good look.

All it takes is a mirror.

That's right. No one has the power to sabotage your efforts at landing and loving your next youth ministry job like you do. So whether you are searching for a youth ministry job or just hoping to stay satisfied in the one you have, the most important skill you will *ever* need is *self-awareness*.

We go to seminars to master our ministry, manage our marriages, and fix our children, but too often we fail to tend to the only common denominator in every single problem we've ever faced: ourselves. Let us give you an example from the real-life world of youth ministry.

We have a friend in ministry who is extraordinary with teenagers. He loves taking them to the deep places, places where they experience God's heartbeat. But he hates "administration." He says it gets in the way of "real ministry."

The problem is not that he hates administration. Most youth workers we know feel the same way. The problem is that instead of learning to dance with the massive administrative needs of his ministry or adding someone to his team who can manage logistics, he's actually moving backward, in a negative spiral. He's grown comfortable blaming his "apathetic" church, his "controlling" senior pastor, and his "half-hearted" volunteers. As a result, the only significant change in his ministry over the past few years has been the increased decibel level of his complaining.

Maybe your story is different. Maybe your need for perfection leads you to spew anger without knowing the collateral damage it produces. Maybe you have such a need for peace and calm that you avoid dealing with little problems until they become huge ones. Maybe you have such an overwhelming drive to be special that you'll do anything—even sabotage your ministry—to avoid being "ordinary."

Jeremiah was right when he wrote, *"The human heart is the most deceitful of all things" (Jeremiah 17:9)*. We each have our own unique brand of self-deception.

The search for the youth ministry job of our dreams begins with self-awareness and a ruthless willingness to know our own brokenness. Thriving in youth ministry begins with becoming an expert at knowing the things about us that everyone close to us knows so well. It begins with relentlessly committing to a deliberate process of growing beyond who we are into more and more of what God made us to be.

MORE THAN KID STUFF

CHAPTER 4

Jed loved working with teenagers, and he was great at it.

He'd shoot baskets all afternoon with a couple of boys, followed by great conversations about life, girls, and faith. He could hang out for hours at a high school football game and never grow tired of spending time with teenagers. Wherever students were, that's where he wanted to be. He was a youth-magnet, loved by students and parents alike.

But in his first full-time youth ministry job (actually his first full-time job of any kind), Jed hated all the administrative work he referred to as "trivial." When the pastor reminded him that part of what he was hired to do was to run the ministry, not just to do the ministry, Jed was convinced that he had a senior pastor that just didn't understand the real world of working with teenagers.

We had an inkling that Jed's days as a paid youth director were numbered when he told us, "You know, this is starting to feel like work. And when it becomes work, it stops being ministry."

Sadly, we were right.

He was off the payroll two months later.

Jed had stepped into his position with a common misconception: "When it becomes work, it stops being ministry."

The truth is, there's a lot of work attached to ministry.

Ask Moses. Ask Noah. And now, you can ask Jed. He was great at the relational stuff—as long as the students came to him. But when the pastor asked him to be accountable for reaching students who didn't show up, or for a 12-month calendar, or for a game plan for training volunteers, Jed simply didn't see those priorities as ministry.

When it was clear that those parts of the job description were simply not going to happen under his leadership, he and the church parted company, leaving dozens of brokenhearted, confused teenagers in his wake.

ANSWER THIS QUESTION FIRST

When Jeff (that co-author of mine you've read so much about) was considering moving from being a volunteer to becoming a paid youth director at his church, I asked him a hard question. "Before you apply," I asked, "which of the following statements describes you better: (1) I want to spend lots of time with teenagers, or (2) I want to manage a ministry that reaches more teenagers than I could reach myself?

"If you choose No. 1," I said, "you'll be happier as an outstanding volunteer at your local church. If you choose No. 2, you're ready to start your search for a professional youth ministry position."

Put another way, are you willing to give up some of time you would spend doing youth ministry in order to *lead* a youth ministry?

THE HIDDEN ASPECTS OF YOUTH MINISTRY

Many first-time youth ministers experience an eye-opening surprise: Sustainable, healthy youth ministries are run by people who spend roughly a third of their time with students, a third of their time with adult volunteers and parents, and a third of their time in a hard chair, reserving vans, updating youth directories, and going to church meetings.

The good news is that when we do ministry this way, we still get to spend lots of time with students. Our friends will still be jealous of this sweet job of ours that actually pays us to hang out with teenagers and have fun. But better still, the team and infrastructures we build will allow our ministries to reach further and deeper than we could ever do alone.

Just because someone is "great with youth" doesn't mean that person will necessarily be a great youth pastor. There's simply a lot of behind-the-scenes work and basic management involved in any sustainable youth ministry.

Every new youth pastor is handed a boxful of expectations from a wide variety of constituencies—from the youth to their parents to the church custodian. Passion and giftedness will simply not be enough, in and of themselves, to overcome a lack of basic leadership skills.

Before you say yes to being a "professional" youth worker, be certain you've taken a good look at all the hidden work it will take to build a sustainable youth ministry. You owe it to the teenagers you will work with to answer that question *before* you get hired.

RECOVERY AND RE-ENTRY

David got caught in the political crossfire. When his pastor and another staff member admitted to an "inappropriate relationship," the entire church launched into chaos.

Though David tried to keep his head down, do his job, and just focus on youth ministry, he couldn't help being drawn into the kind of parking lot conversations that only served to multiply the churn of anxiety. Some people wanted David to become the new pastor, and at the same time, other anxious elders began taking a disproportionate interest in providing "accountability for staff." The word "micromanaging" doesn't begin to do justice to their approach.

In a frenzy of rumors, whispers were heard that the pastor wasn't the only one on staff with "issues" to be dealt with. And because David was the only other full-time staff person left, the indirect accusation was clear as a bell.

Within three months, in a secret elders meeting, a decision was made to fire both the pastor and David. Though there were never any clear accusations against David, he was let go.

Amazingly, David still feels called to youth ministry. But now, besides the disorientation of being unemployed, he now finds himself branded as a "fired youth pastor."

After talking to enough "Davids" and having watched enough of them re-enter their next positions *the wrong way*, we've learned a few things that can prevent David's next youth ministry position from being a repeat of the last situation (or worse). So if you've found yourself in David's position, consider:

1. **Deal with your own stuff first.** If you have people buried in the emotional graveyard of your heart, people for whom you have so much bitterness and resentment that you can no longer talk to them or about them, you may not yet be ready for your next ministry position.

2. **You paid the tuition; don't forget the education.** Some youth pastors have been released from multiple youth ministry positions yet haven't done the serious work of identifying why. Find a friend faithful enough to give you a clear picture of the things you can (and must) change before applying for your next assignment. Are you prepared to steward the vision of your new senior pastor—even if there are some points on which you disagree? Are you ready to deliver the kind of results your church is looking for—before expecting the church to buy into *your* new philosophy of ministry?

3. **You will be blamed for blaming.** In the interview process, remember that few things will be as unattractive as a candidate who blames others for things not working out. How much more appealing is a response like, "My next church will reap the benefits of all I learned from my mistakes at my last church!"

4. **Know what to do differently.** Do your homework to find out for yourself what your previous boss' primary complaints were about you. You can be sure he'll share them in some form with any future employer smart enough to ask.

If you want to be satisfied in your next position, you'll either need to change the way you do ministry or be more discerning when searching for an appropriate fit. Either way, you have the power to change.

THE ABNORMAL
SEARCH

CHAPTER 6

Jim called to let me know he had, for the last month, been searching "with a vengeance" for a new youth ministry position. The climate surrounding his youth ministry had become so toxic that he knew he would be leaving soon, either on his own timetable or involuntarily on someone else's.

I asked, "What have you done so far in the search process?"

He explained, "I've just finished polishing up my résumé."

I waited for the rest of his report.

But he was finished.

He had been "searching *with a vengeance*" for over a month, and all he had done was complete his résumé? (I hated to imagine where he would have been if he had been searching *without* a vengeance!)

When we tell folks that they have not really begun their search process until they have networked with *at least* 100 people, they usually think we're exaggerating. What normal person, they wonder, would do such a thing?

Well, we've learned another name for people who search for youth ministry positions the "normal" way: unemployed.

Sadly, instead of working a deliberate process for discovering their next youth ministry position, most simply hope that, by some unexplainable magic, the job of their dreams will land in their laps.

But there is another way. It starts with an intentional, often tedious, process that can dramatically increase your chances of landing the kind of positions you want. This process all starts with two documents: a timeline and a tracking chart.

Because many (if not most) youth ministry searches are never advertised, relying on standard job posting sites will just not get you very far. The alternative is to use a simple document we've come to call the tracking chart.

SEARCH DOCUMENT #1: CONTACT TRACKING CHART

A tracking chart can be as simple as an Excel document with a column for the person you are contacting, his or her contact information, the date of last contact, the date of your next contact, and a section for notes. (We've included a sample in Appendix B.)

Maybe the importance of a tracking chart will be clearer if we give you a little window into our experience. On average, we'll get a minimum of one call or e-mail each week from someone searching for a youth ministry position. As much as we might like to help, after a few weeks, we forget about almost all but the most recent people we've heard from. The folks who stay on the front burner aren't the ones who only call once but the ones who check in every month or two during their search. Those people stand out for another reason: I can tell they are *working a process*, one of the key skills that will make them successful in a youth ministry position I might recommend them for.

In addition to hearing from people searching for positions, we get almost as many contacts from churches searching for youth pastors. When we get those calls, it is natural that we would think first of those candidates who have contacted us the most recently. As a result, those who work the process are the ones whose résumés we tend to pass along first to searching churches.

SEARCH DOCUMENT #2: YOUR PERSONAL SEARCH TIMELINE

The second document you'll want to create for yourself is a search timeline that can provide you with key benchmarks to hit. The timeline is not built around what you hope other people will do (as in "I'd like to be hired three months from today") but what *you* need to do (as in "I will have made 300 contacts and will have followed up with 100 of them in the next two weeks").

Working your own timeline has a way of keeping your head in the game, especially on those days when it feels like nothing is happening. If you're looking for more detail on what a personal search timeline might look like, we've included a sample search timeline in Appendix A.

If you're like most people we've worked with in the search process, these two documents will jump-start your search in ways that few other methods can, connecting you with searching churches you might never find otherwise.

It sure worked for Ryan (and for my church).

Ryan Wallace graduated in December 2008 from Vanderbilt University. He had plans to head to seminary in the fall, but he had one more semester to stay in town because of a lease on his apartment, so he started looking for a one-semester youth ministry job. He contacted the presbytery executive in our area (the person responsible for connecting and coordinating the efforts of the hundred or so churches in middle Tennessee). He suggested that Ryan contact me to see if I might know of any churches searching.

It just so happened that *we* had an opening for a part-time youth worker, and Ryan fit the bill perfectly. We hired him without ever posting a job opening—almost before we realized that we *had* a job opening. Ryan ended up postponing seminary and moving to a full-time role, staying on our staff for two years.

There's a good chance that the youth ministry job of your dreams may never get posted on anyone's website. In fact, some pastors make it a policy not to post their openings but only to interview people based on personal recommendations.

If you're going to find one of these jobs, you may just have to search a little abnormally.

WEAVING YOUR WEB

CHAPTER 7

In the last chapter, we considered the power of creating your own personal search timeline and developing a contact-tracking document. Let's turn our attention to building a network of contacts that you'll be tracking.

But before we do, we want to first address that biggest "yeah but" that comes up almost every time we talk about this kind of networking: "Yeah, but I just don't know that many people."

Here's the good news: You don't have to know all the people on your contact list in order for them to be extraordinarily helpful to you in your search. In fact, the people you don't know so well can actually be more helpful to you than the people you do know well.

Here's why: Your friends tend to run in the same circles as you and know the same people you know. When you're searching, it's your acquaintances—the friends of friends—who can actually do you the most good.

Here are a few of our favorite places to fish for contacts:

- **Start with your friends in ministry.** Make a list of everyone you know who is currently in ministry or recently was in ministry (this can include senior pastors, youth pastors, youth ministry volunteers, and more). Simply ask each of them to give you the names and contact information of five more ministry contacts. Better yet, invite them to introduce you to those five folks via e-mail. You can ask for that information simply by saying, "Who do you know—anywhere in the country—who is doing great youth ministry or great ministry in general?"

- **Contact denominational or association representatives.** Years ago, when our friend Mary was looking for a youth ministry position in a particular town, I called the denominational exec for that region, who just happened to know of a church that was looking. Within weeks, Mary was hired. This step is crucial if you have particular geographic limitations. If you don't, all the better. You can contact denominational or association representatives all over the country.

- **Tap into existing networks.** Most cities already have an established youth ministry network. Start with the National Network of Youth Ministry (nnym.com). From there, you can use Google® to search for "Youth Ministry Network" and the cities you're interested in. This step alone can put you in touch with hundreds of people who can potentially put you in touch with thousands more.

Let us state the obvious: There are thousands of people looking for youth ministry positions. If you work at intentionally building and working a contact list, you will easily place yourself in the top 10 percent of all those searching. This will not only multiply your chances of finding the youth ministry position you want, it will also give you experience in some of the most important skills you'll need to thrive in the position you actually do get. Skills like:

- Continuing to pursue people you don't yet know

- Working a deliberate process to get you where you want to go

- Persisting in making contacts, even when most people don't call you back

Oh yeah. That last point bears repeating: Don't expect people to immediately call or e-mail you back after just one attempt. Continue to reach out to them until they return your call or e-mail (or ask you not to contact them again).

If you take this process seriously, you'll want to spend time every week calling, e-mailing, or using Facebook® is reach 40 different people a week, tracking the outcome of those contacts, and setting an appropriate follow-up date for each one.

Here's how much we believe in the power of this process: If you will work this process and make 40 contacts each week (20 of which are folks you have not yet contacted) and you haven't been offered a position in six months, we'll refund the price of this book and give you all 300 sessions of our Spice Rack curriculum (a $450 value) absolutely free.

What do you have to lose?

DO YOU HAVE A MATCH?

CHAPTER 8

Sam, the senior pastor of High Point Church, was near despair. "We had no idea that this was going to be such a bad match," he said. Just six months ago, this small congregation was euphoric in welcoming Jae, their first youth pastor, convinced that finally having a full-time youth pastor would turn this consistently struggling youth ministry around. But now, she had resigned, leaving the church stunned and reeling.

A series of awkward and frustrating confrontations had revealed acute differences between Jae and her boss. They differed on such basic things as what "real" worship was, whether outreach or discipleship mattered more, and even whether planning ahead was faithful to the gospel.

"We didn't do a very good job during the interview," Sam admitted. As he recounted the "formal" interview to us, it went something like this:

Sam: "We're just looking for someone who loves Jesus and loves teenagers."

Jae: "Hey, I love Jesus *and* teenagers."

Sam: "Perfect. You're hired!"

Loving Jesus and loving teenagers is not a bad place to start, but it's just that—a *start*. Walking with too many friends through the heartbreak of ministry mismatches has taught us that there's more to the discernment process than just trusting your feelings.

Long-haul youth workers are almost always the ones who take the time to do the hard work of "discerning fit." More than a few eager youth workers jump in with heart wide-open and eyes wide shut, only to discover a few months later that they made a horrible mistake.

So before you put in your first application, take the time to work through the following "fit" questions:

DISCERNMENT QUESTION #1: IN WHAT DENOMINATIONS (INCLUDING NON-DENOMINATIONS) WOULD I BE COMFORTABLE SERVING?

There's a huge difference between worshipping at Grace Bible Church in Alabama and Grace Episcopal in New Jersey.

When we see résumés that say the applicant would be comfortable serving in almost any church—from high-church Episcopalian to hard-core fundamentalist—we know those candidates have not taken the time to answer this question.

Whether we are ready to admit it or not, every one of us has a theology—the way we think and talk about God. And Christians, who all follow the same Savior, can have wildly different ways of thinking and talking about God, the Bible, and the life of discipleship. There's only one starting place for determining whether your theology lines up with the church where you hope to work: You have to take the time to determine out what *yours* is.

Some churches, for example, talk about wanting to "get kids saved" and to "win souls," while others talk about the journey of discipleship or the power of spiritual formation. In some churches, silence, stillness, and reverence are the deepest expressions of worship, while in others, those very same acts communicate deadness and apathy. Even two churches that both describe themselves as "Bible believing" can have very different expressions of what that means.

You need to know what your deal-breaker doctrines are and which ones you can be indifferent or flexible about. If you don't decide beforehand, there's a good chance you'll be going to the mat with your church over things that may not be all that essential to your own theology.

Whether you write it down or talk it through with a friend, mentor, pastor, or spiritual director, knowing your core foundational beliefs about God, the Bible, and ministry will save you and your future church a lot of headache (and heartache) down the road.

If the person or group interviewing you doesn't bring up theology, then be sure that you do. Every church has a set of theological assumptions that they will rightly expect you to not only tolerate but also embrace. You might want to ask questions like these:

- Is there a difference between the way the church sees women and men in ministry?

- In what ways does your church speak about God and Christianity in ways that might be different from other churches in town?

- What kind of person might feel uncomfortable with the theology of the church?

DISCERNMENT QUESTION #2: CAN I REALLY DO THIS JOB?

You'll want to ask whether the job description at a particular church matches your own gifts, talents, and passions. Most youth ministry positions at small or mid-size churches require both administrative and relational proficiency. Can you do both? If not, but you are great at building teams, you can shore up your weak areas with a strong set of volunteers.

If you are the only person on the youth staff, you can be guaranteed that you'll be the one responsible for making sure the vans are rented and the newsletter gets out on time. If you're hoping to spend the vast majority of your time spending time directly with students, you may want to consider whether what you really want is to be a volunteer who supports his or her ministry habit with another job.

DISCERNMENT QUESTION #3: WOULD I ATTEND THIS CHURCH?

We know a youth pastor who spent two years saying, at least weekly, "They just don't know how to worship at this church" before he finally quit. The fact is, they worshipped just fine; it simply wasn't in a form the he could connect with—something he didn't bother to figure out before he signed the contract.

If you're doing a local search, spend a few Sundays at the church you're considering. If you have children, get their impressions, both of the worship and Sunday school. If you're not local, try to arrange your on-site interview over a weekend and attend the service. Many church websites will allow you to view or download videos or MP3s of services and/or sermons.

Before you step into a new situation, you'll want to make sure—as much as you can—that this is a church you can love for a long time. Like in a marriage, you can't know everything about the match, but you can learn enough to know whether you're willing to *choose* to love your partner, even when he or she really gets on your nerves.

MAKE YOUR OWN DEAL-BREAKER LIST

Of course, there are plenty of things you can just get used to in your new church, differences in style and language that may not be your preference but are not deal breakers. But some differences will simply crush your spirit. So before you even start looking, make a short list of deal breakers—things like:

- Style of worship

- Theological assumptions

- Cost of living vs. salary

- Ministry philosophy—for example, a senior pastor who is committed to growth, while you want to focus on small group ministry

- Spousal veto

Be patient if you don't find your fit right away. Despite what the search committee might tell you about its desire for you to "bring change" to the church, remember that it's never a good idea to marry someone assuming they will change.

THE RÉSUMÉ: YOUR FIRST INTERVIEW

CHAPTER 9

I was e-mailed a résumé recently from someone applying for an open position. I loved what I read, but I hated what I saw.

The content was fine. The presentation—well, it looked like it had been done by a third-grader: tiny, almost unreadable fonts; minimal margins; words scrunched together like there was a prize for who could fit the most words on a page. And unfortunately, the appearance communicated volumes.

It gave me my first clue of how this candidate would tend to handle assignments given him in the youth ministry. If his résumé was any indication, he would get the job done but might have trouble finishing well. Fair or not, the typical search committee will assume this candidate wouldn't bring much creative energy beyond first attempts.

Not surprisingly, this candidate never got called for an interview. Here's why.

Your résumé is your first interview. If a search committee considers your résumé (your first impression) embarrassing, there's a good chance you'll never have a chance to make a second one. Those responsible for hiring may simply assume—rightly or wrongly—that your work, your event promotion, and maybe even your judgment would be equally sloppy. A sloppy résumé is like sloppy attire for an interview. You've already spoken volumes before you even open your mouth.

In an age of tremendous publishing software resources built into most computers, there is no excuse for a tacky, amateurish-looking résumé. Take a few extra minutes to make sure your résumé inspires more confidence than questions, more curiosity than contempt.

As you prepare or update your résumé, in addition to giving attention to presentation and accuracy, you'll want to avoid these very avoidable mistakes we've seen more times than we care to count:

- **Cramming.** Somewhere along the way, our candidate with the third-grader résumé must have been told to limit his résumé to no more than one page. That would ordinarily be fine advice, but if following it requires annoyingly small fonts or formatting that makes the eyes squint and the head spin, take two or three pages. Clear and compelling is more important than brief. The one exception to this rule is when a searching church specifically directs applicants to limit their résumés to one page.

- **Meandering.** Your résumé gives your potential employer a quick look at what you have already accomplished. There is no better indication of future success than past success. Those reading your résumé don't need long paragraphs about your philosophy of youth ministry (which will likely sound a lot like 90 percent of the other candidates' paragraphs). What will set you apart is what you have actually done, not what books you have read about what you'd like to do.

- **Not providing a reference from one of your previous churches.** You can be pretty sure that the smart search teams will take the time to check with the senior pastor at any church for which you didn't include a reference. If you want someone other than the senior pastor to be your reference, you'll want to include a raving fan from every church you served in the last 10 to 15 years.

- **Not knowing what your references will say.** Some candidates like to pad their reference list with names of people who might be a little more well known in the world of youth ministry but who really have very little idea of the capacity and gifts of the person they are endorsing. Smart search committees will raise enough good questions to quickly see through these thin references. If you have a reference whom you think might carry more weight in the world of youth ministry, just make sure you help him or her know you well enough to answer common reference questions.

- **Sloppy saving.** You'll want to be careful how you name your résumé document in your computer, especially if you plan to attach your résumé to an e-mail. Attached résumé titles like "Conservative Church Résumé," "Emergent Résumé," and "Ain't I Cool Résumé" may be helpful for your own filing purposes, but good old boring "Nancy Smith's Résumé 1" works best.

ONE FINAL WORD...

With all our hype about the importance of a strong résumé, you might be surprised to hear this one last comment:

We never trust a résumé.

A cool and impressive résumé does not mean that you can do the job any more than a tuxedo on a pig means a great prom date.

So take the time to draft a compelling, results-focused résumé, along with a personal cover letter. But once the résumé is done, spend your time focusing on honing your own craft as a youth ministry practitioner. The writer of Proverbs was right: *Do you see any truly competent workers? They will serve kings rather than working for ordinary people (Proverbs 22:29).*

Landing the youth ministry job of your dreams begins not simply with marketing yourself well but, more importantly, with becoming the youth pastor that your future church is dreaming of.

REFERENCE, PLEASE: AND YOUR MAMA DOESN'T COUNT

CHAPTER 10

When it comes to selecting and preparing references, most youth pastor candidates seem to have only one goal in mind: Do it as quickly as possible!

Not exactly a strategy for success.

This is a book about how to search for a youth ministry position *abnormally*. The fact that you've read this far indicates that you are willing to do this whole search process a little differently from the "normal" (in other words, unemployed and unsatisfied) people.

When it comes to references, the most important abnormal step is this: Use your reference-gathering process as an unparalleled opportunity to grow in self-awareness, which is, you recall from Chapter 1, the most important youth ministry skill *ever*. Instead of leaving a message on your potential reference's voice-mail saying, "I'll be putting you down as a reference. Try to say something nice if a church calls you," you'll be doing something much better.

Assuming that your reference is someone whose opinion you respect (and, of course, he or she shouldn't be a reference if this isn't the case), ask that person for a quick 15-minute phone appointment to go through a few questions like these:

- I'm starting to apply for a few youth ministry positions, and I would love for you to be a reference for me; but just as importantly, I would love your assistance in helping me see my blind spots before I get blindsided by them. I have a few questions, and I'd love your honest feedback. Would that be OK?

- I'm really looking for gaps in my readiness for a position in youth ministry. Could you help?

- If you were looking to hire me at your church, what would give you reason to pause and wonder if I would be a fit for your church?

- Are there any questions a church might ask you about me that you might have trouble answering with enthusiasm?

- Today, if you were in a hiring position, what kind of position would you *not* consider me for?

- Is there anything you have thought about saying to me in the past or in this conversation but you're a little concerned about how to say it? Would you mind sharing it with me?

- If you were in my shoes, where would you focus your efforts in terms of being better prepared for a full-time youth ministry position?

- What are the genuine assets that I bring to a youth ministry position that could differentiate me from other candidates? (You do want to give them some practice saying nice things about you!)

Second, you want to have more references than you need. Ask all your references to write two or three sentences you can include with your résumé. When you come across a tepid endorsement, you can leave that one off.

Third, select a balanced set of references: parents, pastors, supervisors, professors, even youth who might have been in your program in the past. Leave off your spouse or family members, knowing that most search committees will assume that family recommendations are naturally inflated.

Remember, too, that your Facebook® page is an electronic résumé, whether you like it or not. So if you have friends who like to post inappropriate pictures on your wall, you'll want to hide those friends from public view. Though it may seem far-fetched, we have seen churches rescind a job offer based on the indiscretion a candidate showed by what he or she included on his or her Facebook® page.

You'll want to think like a savvy search team that is desperate not to get burned *again* by hiring the wrong person. So take the time to check your references before someone else does.

CHECK YOUR FLY

CHAPTER 11

One of the many benefits of getting older is that you have a much larger reservoir of mistakes that others can learn from. Here's one of mine.

I had just finished making a consulting proposal to a church's board of elders. The interview took place in a small parlor at the church, with comfortable couches and overstuffed chairs arranged in a circle. And for most of the hour and a half presentation, I was leaning forward on the edge of the soft chair I had been assigned.

I had presented with a nice balance of informed candor and relaxed humor. The questions the group had asked were all right in my wheelhouse. As the meeting was wrapping up, I felt like I had hit it out of the park, that is until...

We all rose to stand in a circle to pray together, and the church's senior pastor—a longtime friend, the one who had invited me to present to the elders—stepped across the small circle and gave me a big hug. It seems like a strong display of affection following a consulting proposal, but I just assumed that I must have been even better than I thought. As I smiled and muttered a quiet "you're welcome," my friend whispered very quietly, "Now might be a good time to zip up your fly."

Yes, I fully "briefed" the elders that night. And no, we didn't get the job.

SOME QUESTIONS DON'T GET SPOKEN

Your résumé might get you an interview, but once you're on site, wise interviewers are watching far more than your words. They are watching your smile, your folded arms, your energetic engagement, or your aloof demeanor. Here are a few of the questions search committees want answered in every interview, but these questions will almost never be voiced:

- Does she fit in here?

- Will my son like her?

- Does he like us?

- Can she engage both youth and adults?

- Does she greet everyone in the room?

- How's his energy level?

- How will his spouse fit in here?

- Can I trust him with my teenager?

Some of these questions might make you cringe or might seem unfair, but don't kid yourself—they are being asked.

It's possible, too, that your first impression might be made before you ever appear on the church property. There's a good chance someone will do some background research on you prior to the interview. So before the formal interview, take a minute to type your name into Google and see what first impression the rest of the world might be getting about you.

DOES WHAT I WEAR REALLY MATTER?

The short answer is…yes.

It is not uncommon for gifted, experienced candidates to be immediately written off in the first five minutes of an interview, just because of how they are dressed. Of course, because churches are so different in their "normal" attire, there are no one-size-fits-all rules for how to dress for an interview. But if you show up wearing a rumpled shirt and dusty shoes—

what might be your "normal" Sunday outfit—when interviewing for a position at a church filled with teenagers who wear khakis and button-downs, you might as well wear a sign that says, "I didn't care enough to try to understand your church."

On the other hand, we've never known anyone who lost a job because he or she dressed too nicely for the interview. There's nothing wrong with asking before you arrive, "How will people be dressed for the interview?" When the answer comes back, "We are very casual around here," you will want to get a little definition. For some people, "casual" is a stained white T-shirt and warm-up pants, while for others it is having a sport coat that doesn't match the pants. Remember, you're not dressing just for any students who might be in the interview; you are dressing for those who will be interviewing you.

WORKING THE ROOM

In every setting during the interview (especially the informal get-to-know-you gatherings), think of yourself as the host of the party, with responsibility for making everyone feel welcome. It's always your turn to take the first step and introduce yourself.

This orientation may be especially hard for introverts who, after a long day of traveling and meetings, just want to sit on a comfy couch and relax. But your interviewers are (rightly) observing your initiative and how intentionally you connect with a variety of people: the students, the parents, and the other staff.

Remind yourself that every person there has at least one good story, and the game is to discover at least one each from as many people in the room as possible. Ask about their families, their church, the youth ministry, their education, and their jobs. If you're curious, it won't be long until you hit on something fascinating. You can rest later.

REMEMBER ME

You want to leave an impression in your interview, but remember that people are seldom impressed with people who are trying to be impressive.

You may have heard the story of Lady Randolph Churchill, mother of former British Prime Minister Winston Churchill. She is said to have remarked when comparing British politicians William Gladstone and Benjamin Disraeli as statesmen and dinner party companions, "After sitting next to Gladstone during dinner, I felt like I sat next to the most clever man in all of England. But after sitting next to Disraeli, I felt like I was the most clever woman in England" (paraphrasing from Christopher Hibbert, *Disraeli: A Personal History*).[3]

When you take the time to learn about the church and the people who are interviewing you, it counts. When the search committee asks, "Do you have any questions for us," and you have nothing to ask, it plants the seed that you might just be disinterested in talking about anything but yourself.

Practice learning names, even if it's hard for you. Especially if it's hard. Remembering names and a little something about each person communicates that you just might have the initiative and relational bandwidth to care for students with whom it might be hard to connect.

Before arriving, take a little time to know the church by digging around in the church's website. In the phone interviews, get to know any unique struggles the church is having in the youth ministry.

Be prepared to answer the questions you know will come by having a few stories about your ministry experience ready to share—you might skip the stories about the water balloon wars in the sanctuary or duct-taping the senior pastor to his bunk at camp. Be prepared to tell a story about how you saw God in the life of a teenager or how the church rallied for a fantastic youth event. Make the focus less about how great you are and more about "this fantastic volunteer" or "a teenager I was really proud of."

So be intentional about your dress, pay attention to people personally, and remember that the most important questions may never get asked, only observed. And oh yeah…check your fly.

BE YOURSELF—BUT DON'T OVERDO IT

Jake was a top-three candidate at Main Street Chapel, a conservative, small-town church. He was in his mid-30s, and the leaders of the church were glad to have someone older applying for the job. Jake played guitar and even had a CD out. He had long hair and was a little edgy, and the church liked that about him.

He called it like he saw it. Some people on the committee appreciated his candor, while the more conservative members thought he needed a tighter filter between brain and mouth. But they all agreed to take him off the list when one dad asked, "What do you struggle with?"

Jake answered matter-of-factly with one word: "Lust." No explanation. Just one awkward word that hung in the air for an uncomfortably long time.

For Jake (and for most honest Christian men), this was a totally truthful answer. But sometimes we can be so transparent that all we accomplish is making team members squirm in their seats. If you are trying to weed out churches that don't appreciate your call-it-like-it-is demeanor, this kind of discomfort-creating response will work for you. But if you hope to move forward in the process, you'll want to nuance your answers.

Not all "I'm-just-being-honest" mistakes are as obvious as this one, but they can be just as deadly. We've observed a few interview-killer statements that seem to get repeated again and again:

"My last job was awful."

Some people are tempted to show how smart they are by talking about how dumb their old coworkers (and bosses) were. They say things like, "I like your church because the parents are involved. At my last church, you couldn't move the parents with a snowplow." Or "My old pastor, bless his heart, just didn't understand what discipleship is all about. It was sad, really."

It doesn't take a leap of logic to realize that if you are full of complaints about your previous church, it won't be long before you are full of complaints about your new church. You, after all, will be the common denominator.

"Hey, the '70s called, and they want that shirt back."

Negative humor and sarcasm may have become a mainstay for many insecure youth ministers, but that style typically yields lousy interview results. You simply don't know those you are meeting well enough to know whether they will find your cutting humor charming or deeply offensive. You can be pretty sure, though, that both types will be in the room.

"Excuse me while I take this call."

Unless you have a terminally ill family member or a wife about to give birth, we recommend that you simply turn off your phone for the hour or two of the interview. If you absolutely must, you can always discretely check for messages during natural breaks.

Typically the generation that is interviewing you lives by this mantra: "Friends don't let friends text during dinner." Even checking the phone to see who's calling sends a negative message to most professionals. It says to them in so many words, "I sure hope the person calling me is more interesting than you are."

ONE FINAL IT-SHOULD-GO-WITHOUT-SAYING WARNING

A youth pastor friend finished up his final round of a grueling series of interviews, and it seemed clear to everyone that this job was his if he wanted it. No formal offer had been made, but there was a clear handshake understanding that inking the deal would just be a formality.

That night, the candidate returned to the home where he was staying, the home of the chair of the search committee. Now, this person just happened to own a "wine and spirits" distributorship, and he offered the soon-to-be staff member a drink to celebrate. The two of them had become quite good friends, or so it seemed to the candidate, so he enjoyed a drink with someone he was sure would be one of his closest friends as he launched his ministry.

During the two hours of relaxing, our youth pastor friend returned to the home's well-stocked bar at least five times, enough to make the chair of the search committee begin to wonder if they were making the right decision. A week of long and painful deliberations later, the church rescinded its offer and continued its search.

Be yourself, but remember there are authentic ways of being yourself around your closest friends and family that might be different from appropriately being yourself around those you are just getting to know. Be yourself. But don't overdo it.

HOW TO TELL IF A SEARCH COMMITTEE IS LYING

CHAPTER 13

The old joke goes something like this:

Question: How do you know if members of the search committee are lying?

Answer: Their lips are moving.

It's cynical maybe, but it makes you wonder how old jokes get started. Maybe it's because too many people have had an experience like our friend Tyrone.

Tyrone took a small pay cut to be associate pastor at Grace Church, but it was worth it. The search committee had told him he would have "no management responsibilities." He would just preach and create an outreach ministry, his two sweet spots. Tyrone felt like it was too good to be true.

He signed on the dotted line, and as he was unpacking boxes in his office on day one, his pastor said, "After you get settled in, let me introduce you to the people who will be working for you." Within weeks, Tony discovered that he not only was managing a staff of three; he also had dozens of volunteers "under his umbrella," volunteers he was expected to inspire, coordinate, and, of course, manage.

How does something like that happen?

THE REST OF THE STORY

It's not that search committee members were lying actually. They were telling the truth they understood. They simply didn't know the nuances that Tyrone's boss, the senior pastor, had in his mind. With nothing on paper, the search team and the pastor had two different pictures of what was needed in this job. The expectations were spelled out with a broad brush (for example, "create an outreach ministry") and details were developed by an intuitive word-of-mouth process.

If the church you are working with doesn't provide you with a written job description before you arrive for the interview, it would be wise for you to send a note outlining what you believe you would be hiring you to do. Your job description draft could just bring to light two (or more!) very different perceptions of the position.

Our buddy Brent was never told that he was expected to be the coach of the church's elementary school soccer team. But he sure found out when parents started calling with their children's jersey sizes and asking about when the first practice would be. It was just the way the church "had always done it," and no one seemed to think of it during the interview and hiring process.

THE WHOLE TRUTH

Patti ran into a different kind of problem at her new church. It wasn't what was left out of the conversation; it was what she actually heard. Her pastor had enthusiastically expressed during the interview process, "Patti, if you come here, you'll have a blank slate. You can build your dream youth ministry on *your* vision."

But when Patti began bringing in unchurched students by the dozens, most of whom had no idea how to "behave in church," the church's leadership, including the senior pastor, told her to cut it out. "What happened to my *blank slate*?" she began to wonder, with growing bitterness. "Why did they lie to me?"

Few senior pastors or search committees shade the truth on purpose. They, like you, are simply putting their best foot forward. Just like in any relationship, you can't possibly ask enough of the right questions to avoid being surprised later in the relationship (take marriage, for example). And even if you could, institutions—like people, when they are healthy—have a way of growing and evolving over the years, making many of the assumptions of a few years ago no longer true.

It is your job, though, to explore the church's culture so you can learn as much as you can about the likes, dislikes, and unspoken traditions—especially ones they may "forget" to mention.

ASKING GOOD QUESTIONS

Committee members will be as accurate as they can be, but many things will just naturally get left out of the conversation. So you'll want to add the following questions to your growing list:

- What are some beloved traditions of the church?

- Has the church ever considered _____ (your favorite ministry idea)?

- How do you see the youth pastor's mix of in-office and out-of-office time?

- What are the biggest challenges facing the youth ministry?

- Three years from now, what would you like to see different about the youth ministry?

- And what would you like to see stay the same?

Remember, there's a very good chance that you've done more interviews than those who are interviewing you. So show a little grace if they don't seem to give the full story. With good questions, you can limit the surprises. But you'll never be able to ask enough questions to cover every eventuality, so be prepared—without bitterness—for the organic changes to the expectations of your job.

SELLING WITHOUT SOUNDING LIKE A SALESPERSON

CHAPTER 14

(DON'T LOOK OUT ONLY FOR YOUR OWN INTERESTS, BUT TAKE AN INTEREST IN OTHERS, TOO. YOU MUST HAVE THE SAME ATTITUDE THAT CHRIST JESUS HAD (PHILIPPIANS 2:4-5).)

Youth pastors interviewing for a new position have a dilemma.

We know we need to differentiate ourselves from every other candidate, but the last thing we want to do is come off as arrogant and self-serving. We want the church to "buy," but we really don't want to "sell."

Maybe we could take a lesson from my visits to my doctor. I'm always buying, but he's never selling. How does he do it?

Picture the scene. You're in one of the chilly examination rooms, reading old magazines, when the doctor comes in. He smiles and simply asks how you're doing. You might start with some polite chitchat, but pretty soon, you're telling the doctor about what's been bothering you. Maybe he pokes around a little bit.

"Where does it hurt?" he asks.

You tell him where it hurts. He listens and asks a few more questions.

"That sounds like XYZ," he says. "I've got something that should take care of it for you." He then suggests a prescription or a set of procedures or exercises. And we "buy."

THINKING LIKE A DOCTOR; THINKING LIKE ARCHITECTS

What if we approached interviews the same way: asking good questions, finding out where it hurts, and explaining how the problem might be solved?

Sometimes, there's nothing clearly broken, but the church does have dreams of what the future could hold. In this case, you ask the architect's question: "What would you like to build?"

Either way, it is important that you take the time to listen; don't jump too quickly to a simplistic solution (one they have likely already tried). A good doctor asks follow-up questions to make sure the diagnosis is correct.

If leaders at the church say they want "more teenagers to have a closer relationship with God," you can ask, "What might that look like for you?" It usually takes four to seven follow-up questions to get to the heart of their concerns. Try to spend twice as much time asking questions and listening as you do giving answers.

Asking diagnostic questions, like those below, allows you to differentiate yourself without sounding like a salesperson:

- What are some words you would use to describe your church?

- If a genie granted you one wish, what would you wish for your youth ministry?

- Is there anything that worries or concerns you about the future of the youth ministry?

- If you had all the money and help you needed to "renovate" the youth ministry, what features would you want to preserve and what would you want to fix or change?

When you take this approach to "selling," search committee members will likely see a caring, insightful person who just might have solutions to the specific problems they are facing. When you care about who they are first, you communicate that you are willing to partner with the church to fulfill its dreams rather than coming in as a lone ranger to fulfill your dream of getting a job in youth ministry.

OVERCOMING THE "THEY NEVER CALLED BACK" EXCUSE

CHAPTER 15

Carlos had been looking for a job for months. He was tired and frustrated. Most churches never bothered checking back with him. He had no idea whether his résumé had landed in the "love him" pile or the "leave him" pile.

"These are churches," he said to his friends. "You'd think they'd have the common courtesy to get back with you."

So he gave up. He quit sending out inquiries. He didn't even look for new job postings. It was too aggravating. Then one weekend, in a burst of desperate energy, he sent out dozens of e-mails. Every church that looked even remotely interesting received an inquiry asking for more information.

A few days later, he'd received no responses. "Typical!" he thought. Now he was mad. He'd had it with churches and their incompetence. He made the following post on his Facebook wall:

"I just sent out 75 résumés to 75 churches and not one has responded. What's wrong with these people!?"

MANAGING THE PROCESS

Let's start by stating the obvious: Most churches run their youth pastor searches poorly. Most search committees (if the church takes the time to have one) are made up of well-intentioned, overcommitted volunteers, most of whom have never participated in a search like this before. Other searches are run entirely by stretched-way-too-thin senior pastors who manage the search in between all the other responsibilities of running the church.

If you've ever worked with volunteers or senior pastors (and if you haven't, it's time to start), you know how it goes. Sometimes the execution is stellar and blows you away, but it can definitely be a hit or miss proposition.

Even though grumbling and scowling may provide a brief (and we might add "useless") emotional release, it won't get you any closer to a job. What will get you closer to the job of your dreams is for you to take responsibility for being efficient and organized, even when churches are not. It may not necessarily be fair, but it's often one of the biggest differences between an employed youth pastor and an unemployed one.

Though those hiring you may not know it, your initiative is part of what differentiates you in the hiring process. A candidate who consistently follows up with the search team or senior pastor is clearly going to be more memorable than the garden-variety candidate who sends a résumé and waits.

Don't be offended by the lack of return phone calls or e-mails. Some search committees don't meet more than every other week, and some don't even meet that often. And often those teams are inundated with a pile of résumés that all come in at the same time, making it more likely that yours will be ignored.

Those who work a deliberate search process will stand out head and shoulders above ordinary wait-and-see candidates. If you want to move beyond an anemic search toward landing the job you will love, you can start with this checklist:

- ☐ Create a tracking list (described in Chapter 6) of all the churches, contact names, and information, plus the date of the contact and the any response received.

- ☐ If you don't get a response in two weeks, resend your e-mail "in case the first one didn't reach you." It's OK to ask about their time schedule for the process.

- ☐ Check back with the church about once every two or three weeks. Ask, "Is there any more information I can supply you?" Comment on something you might have seen in their church newsletter or website. One out of 10 churches will be annoyed by your follow-up, but most will appreciate your diligence.

- ☐ Send an immediate thank you note to anyone who contacts you. Remember, it's OK at any point to ask about the timing of their next step.

- ☐ Don't assume they are not interested just because you haven't heard back. Church committees tend to be hybrid creatures: slow-moving and fast-acting at the same time. They can drag out the process for months and then suddenly want you to come in for an interview in three days.

- ☐ If there's a position or two that you are very interested in, it's OK to let those churches know if you have started the interview process with another church.

- ☐ Don't stop sending out résumés and interviewing until you have written confirmation of being hired. You want to be sure you have a deal before you announce it to everyone.

IF YOU STILL DON'T HEAR BACK...

If you're listening eagerly for a reply and you only hear silence from all corners, it's time to take a look at what message you are sending to churches. Maybe they're not replying because there is something about your résumé or first contact that has failed to make a good first impression (see Chapters 6-10). Take the time to contact a friend whose business savvy you respect, and ask for an honest review of your résumé and your cover letter.

Or maybe your social networking page, your blog, or your website is broadcasting to search committees, "Danger, Will Robinson!" If a search committee had looked at Carlos' Facebook postings during his job search, most of his posts were about how tired he was and how the world wasn't treating him right.

Churches will be notoriously slow getting back to you. But if you are different, you will stand out. If you work a deliberate, robust search plan and every single one of the 75 churches you contacted has failed to respond for several months, you can follow the steps outlined in Chapter 4 and launch a healthy self-assessment to get you moving forward again.

FAMILY MATTERS

CHAPTER 16

Does your spouse *want* you to be a youth worker?

Sean was a popular youth volunteer who was having a tough time at his retail job. He decided he was ready to it throw in the towel at the store and finally apply for the open youth director position at his church. His wife, who volunteered with him every Sunday night, just smiled and said, "If that's what you think you need to do...."

Sean was having lunch with his mom one afternoon when she dropped a bomb: "You know, don't you, that Brenda doesn't want you to leave your retail job?"

"What?" Sean said. "She never said that."

"Of course she didn't. She loves you."

Over dinner that night, Sean brought up the question to his wife gently, "Wanna hear something crazy? My mom thinks you don't want me to apply for this job."

"I never said that," she said hesitantly.

This time, Sean was attentive enough to see the seeds of doubt he'd been ignoring in his wife. After the long conversation, they decided together that this was actually not the right time for their family to experience new stress, less money, and big change.

Because our spouses want us to be happy, they might not always put all their concerns and fears on the table. Before you send out the first application, you will want to have several long conversations with your spouse about the impact of moving into a first full-time ministry position or from your current ministry into a new ministry altogether. At the very least, you'll want to talk through the three most common concerns we hear from youth ministry spouses:

WILL THE FAMILY SEE YOU OFTEN ENOUGH?

The intensity of this question ratchets up exponentially once there are children in the house. A husband or wife might be willing deal with a little loneliness, but few will stand for their children being ignored. Before starting a new position, take time to realign your priorities and your schedule, to get crystal clear about what day(s) and times you plan to protect as no-ministry zones, and to determine what evenings will designated as family time (where you unplug from ministry). We offer a little guidance for developing a "Rhythmic Week" at YMArchitects.com.

The wife of a youth pastor in transition captured the sentiment of many ministry spouses facing a move when she said, "I just want you to understand that I'm grieving, and this move is going to be hard for me." Making yourself consistently available for your spouse through a deliberate schedule of time together just might prevent your new position from being worse than the one before it.

WILL WE HAVE TO MOVE?

If you are involved in a national search, keep in mind that you're not the only one who will be changing jobs and missing friends. If your spouse is the primary breadwinner, the process becomes even more complicated, and you might need to limit your search to something local or regional. If you do have more flexibility in relocation, decide together, before sending the first application, what "deal-breaker" parameters, if any, you will have: parts of the country (or world), kind of church, minimum salary, type of city or town, and so on.

CAN WE AFFORD IT?

It's not only OK to talk about the money question together—it's imperative. We've seen candidates get far down the road interviewing with a church, only to find that the church is offering a salary that is dramatically lower than what they can afford to live on. Rather than taking a job and then becoming resentful that the church is not taking care of you appropriately, you'll want to get clarity on the front end—both about how much your family will need to live on and how much the church is willing to pay. It doesn't help you or the church for you to pretend you can live on a salary you can't.

KEEP TALKING

Remember Sean and his reluctant wife? Two years later, the position at church came open again. This time, things at home had stabilized and Sean's wife encouraged him to apply. He asked if she was sure, and this is what she said: "This change is going to lower our income, change your schedule, and give our family more attention than I'd like to have at church. But because I'm not worried about any of those things, I think that this time, it must be God's plan for us." And Sean is still in that position today.

Youth ministry is hard enough when your spouse is totally on board. It can be overwhelming when he or she is not.

HOLY HESITATION

CHAPTER 17

Mike had a good job when he sensed that God might be calling him into full-time ministry. At first, it felt pretty amazing. But just when he was ready to commit, his doubts stopped him in his tracks.

"Maybe it's not really God."

"I'm not a great speaker."

"I'm not really the kind of guy people expect to represent God."

"Maybe I'm just running from the job I don't like more than being called to ministry."

"I'm not sure what I think about the whole idea of 'hearing' from God!"

He made a pro-and-con list—with nothing in the pro column!

But God seemed to keep nudging in ways Mike couldn't ignore. He went on to do a fantastic job in a very difficult ministry assignment. He actually became rather famous.

OK, his name wasn't Mike. It was Moses.

"Holy hesitation" seems to be part of most real calls to ministry, whether it's Jonah, the disciples, or you and me. Ask 10 people about how they got into ministry, and more than five of them will tell you they resisted.

Often, our hesitation centers on our sense of inadequacy, around the notion that this job is too big for us. If that's your concern, we have some comforting news for you: You're right. You can't do it.

That very awareness is the first step to launching into a healthy ministry, fully aware of your need for grace. Holy hesitation is just a wise realization that faithful ministry can only be accomplished through God's power and on God's terms. Not a bad way to start.

In fact, one veteran senior pastor who has worked with many, many young pastors over the years told us that he *always* looks for hesitation in people pursuing ministry. "The ones who are over-eager," he says, "the ones who say 'I can do this!' are the ones who make me nervous."

The way some people talk about discerning God's will, you would assume that God's will is always accompanied by a "peaceful, easy feeling." But this is God, not the Eagles. This is the God famous for calling people out of their comfort zones and upsetting the apple cart of otherwise stable and steady lives.

BUT...

Sometimes, though, the bad feeling in the pit of your stomach is not just "holy hesitation" or evidence that it really is God calling. Sometimes, an ongoing uneasiness might just point to the possibility that this particular direction is not a fit for you. Maybe the timing is wrong. Maybe this church is just not a match for your gifts. Or just maybe God has other plans for you.

We hesitate to make a list of questions to ask in this process simply because discernment is so much more textured than a checklist. At the end of the day, after practicing discernment and seeking out wise, godly counsel, we are daily called to walk boldly uncertainty, trusting that God can and will redirect when necessary.

When Mother Teresa was asked by a visitor to Calcutta for her prayers, she, of course, responded with willingness, "...and how would you like me to pray for you?"

The man responded, "Pray that I have clarity about what I am to do next."

Mother Teresa's response shocked him: "That is one thing I cannot pray for you."

The man was incredulous. "And why is that?"

"To have clarity," said Mother Teresa, "is to be free of the need to trust. I will pray for trust, but I cannot pray for clarity."

May you step with trust into the confident uncertainty of God's unfolding call on your life.

HOW TO LOCK IN YOUR YOUTH MINISTRY DREAM JOB

———————— SECTION TWO ————————

During the recent Great Recession, we asked our friend Steve Schneeberger, the executive director of Florida's Youth Ministry Institute, this question: "How can youth pastors make sure that they're not the first ones laid off when the church is forced to make tough staffing decisions?"

His answer was unqualified and quick: "Become indispensable."

Being "indispensable" is, of course, hard to define, but most of us can spot an indispensable youth worker when we see one. The fact is, we are all replaceable. A well-run youth ministry is not led by a lynchpin superstar. It's run by a master architect who has built the team and infrastructure that will allow the ministry to thrive even after the inevitable day when the youth pastor leaves. In the pages that follow in this section, we will coach you through some of the keys to locking in your position and becoming an indispensable youth pastor.

If you've just landed a position in youth ministry, congratulations! As far as we're concerned, it's the best gig in the world. So we'd love to help you keep your job for as long as you and God had in mind when you were called. We've written this section (the next 18 chapters) specifically with you in mind.

We've walked with way too many youth pastors and churches that wound up parting ways in painful and unpleasant ways. We've also both done things that either nearly got us fired or created so much negativity that we wished we had been. In almost every premature departure of a youth pastor we have seen, there have been a few common denominators. We've collected them here, knowing that the smartest way to learn from mistakes is to learn from someone else's.

If you've already landed your current position, you may have skipped the first section entirely. This is the point when we ask you to go back before you take the next step. Take a few minutes to read (or reread) Chapters 1-4 right now, since they set the stage for wisely locking in your current position, for becoming indispensable.

We'll start this section with a few war stories of avoidable conflicts youth pastors have experienced. Even when the battles didn't result in the youth pastor's departure, the ripple effects of church conflict are potentially heartbreaking for the family, the church, and the students—perhaps most heartbreaking because much of the most toxic conflict can be avoided.

The good news is, we've also seen hundreds of youth ministry veterans walk deftly through the field of potential land mines and come out thriving on the other side. Their secrets to success are here, too.

Now that you've landed your dream youth ministry job, let's lock it in.

CLARITY IS JOB ONE

CHAPTER 18

Within a few years of starting my new youth ministry position, way back in the '80s, I had moved into full cold-war tactics with my senior pastor. I was convinced that he had unrealistic expectations that he seldom, if ever, shared with me. He, on the other hand, was tired of being ambushed by unhappy parents who seemed to come to him in a steady stream, all sharing their concerns about the youth ministry.

It all came to a head one day in my senior pastor's office when he said in frustration, "I just need to know what's going on with the youth ministry!"

To which I responded with no little energy, "Ask me anything you want! I'll be *happy* to tell you!" I followed up by introducing him to a little biblical notion I wanted him to ponder. I said, "If these people are so unhappy about the youth ministry, why don't you have them come to *me* and talk about it rather than going first to my boss—isn't that what the Bible says we should do?!"

I was right of course, at least about what the Bible says *other people* should do. But I was totally blind to what I needed to be doing differently. I was assuming that *if only* the rest of the people in the church would act like Christians, all my ministry problems would go away.

I was missing a key piece required of anyone who wants to firmly establish a ministry, and in the process, I was hurting myself without even knowing it.

What was I missing?

It's a simple truth, really: Clarity is *my* job.

Here's what I mean.

CLARITY WITH MY SENIOR PASTOR

It was my job to keep my pastor updated on the decisions I was making, especially the ones that he would eventually hear about from angry parents, frustrated leaders, or disappointed students. Failing to take responsibility for those updates (actually, it might be better to call them "warnings") set my pastor up to be criticized without giving him any information to the contrary.

I realize now that when people complain to a senior pastor, they are almost always asking, "…and what are *you* going to do about it?" My pastor's sometimes-confrontational conversations with me were only an expression of trying to support his flock.

The sad fact is that it would have taken very little effort for me to have kept my boss updated and prepared for the questions that were certain to come his way. But instead of preparing him, I chose to complain that he was getting in my way, not letting me do my job.

CLARITY ABOUT SHIFTS IN EXPECTATIONS

Clarity is also our job when it comes to dealing with unexpected shifts in expectations. Roughly 100 percent of youth workers discover in the first year in their new positions that the church has expectations that are actually different from those shared in the interview process. And in our experience, roughly 95 percent of those youth workers do little more than complain about the shifts in expectations.

If you discover that the expectations being placed on you have shifted, you can midwife clarity by meeting with your supervisor and saying something like this: "When I interviewed, I heard _____ as the most important priority of my position. I'm picking up that actually _____ may be a higher priority in your mind and in the mind of the church leadership. Am I reading the cues correctly?"

You may learn that there has been vision drift, and you give your senior pastor the chance to reaffirm the original priority. Or it may be that your boss will want to nuance the expectation a bit. The key is for us to take the responsibility to clarify those expectations—and to avoid the complaining passivity, the response of "normal" youth workers. And remember, this is a conversation you'll likely need to have every year or so as the priorities of your position naturally shift.

CLARITY WITH NEGATIVE TRIANGLES

One other context in which the clarity principle holds true relates to those criticizers who "triangle" their concerns by talking to everyone *but* the person they have concerns with. We can waste lots of energy blaming people for talking negatively about us before talking to us directly. But blaming doesn't move us forward. It is singularly unhelpful to expect anxious people *not* to talk in triangles. And blaming them simply keeps us stuck in an unproductive dance of negativity.

What *is* helpful is to recognize that people not coming to us doesn't prevent us from going directly to them. We don't have to agree with them to understand their point of view. By listening with appreciative curiosity, we can gain clarity about their concerns, making sure we understand, without defending or justifying. Parents particularly need to know we are on their side, more than we are trying to get them on *our* side.

Typically, a parent bringing criticism doesn't care primarily about our model or our new initiative or even the theological underpinnings of our ministry. Almost every complaining parent I've ever met wants his or her child to have a more positive experience in the youth ministry. Not an unreasonable expectation.

By partnering with parents to develop strategies for engaging their children in healthy ways, we can get on the same side of the table with parents and step off of the worrisome treadmill of debating about program styles and schedules.

You may be thinking, "How can I talk with them if I don't know who they are?" Fair enough. You might not be able to talk directly to every person who is out there secretly criticizing your program, but you can get pretty close. Just make a list of the folks you think might be unhappy with what's going on in your ministry, and meet with them. At the end of the meeting, just ask, "Is there anyone else that I should meet with or whose concerns you think I should know about?" You'll get to almost all your detractors.

The art of building clarity with our leaders, our volunteers, our parents, and our supervisors can be time-consuming business, at least on the front end—but not nearly as time-consuming as not doing it.

TICKET FOR THE CLUE TRAIN

CHAPTER 19

Here's a little secret.

There is a subtle skill your church will expect from you, one you will likely never see on a job description. With it, you will anticipate little problems before they become big ones. Without it, you may meet every formal expectation in your job and still find yourself on the short end of your annual evaluation.

Tad was called to be a youth pastor in a new church after years of experience. In each church he served, he could point to healthy numbers of youth and leaders participating. But he was dogged, in every church he served, by unfortunate disagreements with senior pastors, who all, he argued, gave mixed messages about what they really wanted.

In one conversation with us, his current senior pastor told us, "I like Tad. I really do. But there are so many times when he just doesn't 'get it.' He just doesn't seem to have intuitive leadership."

Intuitive leadership. It's a hard-to-define term, a combination of social intelligence and creative initiative, and a first-class ticket for the clue train. Though it's hard to define, youth pastors without it face an uphill climb and find themselves scratching their heads about why so many people have so many unrealistic expectations.

The intuitive leader reminds me a little bit of Jesus' parable of the talents. You remember how in that story, two of the servants took the master's money and brought their master a nice return on his investment. They practiced intuitive leadership. They didn't wait for their master to prescribe every step of the *how*. The master expected his servants to fill in lots of gaps in the process of achieving profitable results. He fully expected them to see what needed to be done and do those things, without waiting for explicit instructions to be given.

The third servant, you remember, followed only the instructions he had been given and met the bare minimum expectations. He hid his talent in the ground, bringing his master no return on his investment. Without intuitive leadership, he was shocked to see the money taken away from him and given to the intuitive leaders around him.

The intuitive leader is intensely results-driven.

I know talk of "results" in ministry may sound horribly unspiritual, but when we get more spiritual than the Bible, there's a good chance we have missed something in the translation. Remember, in addition to the parable of the talents, Jesus was consistently clear in his expectation that his disciples "bear fruit" (John 15).

In the similar way, those who invest in you as a youth pastor are expecting a return on their investment. In six months or a year, they don't care how many staff meetings you went to or how many reports you wrote or how cool your model of youth ministry is. They will want to know if their investment in you has given them a more stable, sustainable youth ministry and whether the ministry has more deeply impacted the lives of the next generation and their families.

Intuitive leaders don't wait for instructions to be given; they gather the information they need and take the next steps forward. When intuitive leaders know that they need more information from their supervisors before moving forward, they own the responsibility to gather that information, even if it requires daily reminders to the boss.

Intuitive leaders still accomplish the responsibilities on their job description. It's not that they are simply gut-level, shoot-from-the-hip people. They go beyond their job descriptions, solving problems that might never have been anticipated.

Intuitive leaders don't make excuses for why things aren't working but develop solutions and take the initiative to recommend solutions to the appropriate supervisors or boards, the kinds of solutions that keep moving the ministry forward.

Intuitive leaders are relentless learners. They embrace Malcolm Gladwell's principle that it takes at least 10,000 hours (about five years of full-time work) in a particular field before you can become an expert.[4] Intuitive leaders don't simply assume that because they have "successful" experience that they have all the answers, so they keep learning.

Intuitive leaders read well between the lines:

- They know if and when to remove their piercings in respect for the generation they are meeting with

- They know when to ask challenging questions and when to keep silent

- They take responsibility when programs don't work and seem to have a game plan for moving the ministry forward

The intuitive leader recognizes that not every reasonable expectation is spoken and, as a result, will likely hear the most important evaluation of all: "Well done, good and faithful servant."

EVOLUTION, NOT REVOLUTION

Let's say you are at a national youth convention, listening to a brilliant speaker, and you have an epiphany. You suddenly decide that small groups are the ultimate solution to developing faithful disciples. But sadly, you realize that your youth ministry has absolutely no small groups. And let's say, just for the sake of argument, you happen to be exactly right—that a small-groups-based strategy is *exactly* what's needed.

You are so fired up about this plan that you come back from the convention and announce to everyone involved in the youth ministry:

"Hey guys! We're scrapping the whole fun-and-games approach to Wednesday nights. We all know it's nothing more than glorified babysitting anyway. Instead, we are going to start going deep, developing community where we can be real, and launching a brand-new small groups ministry next week! You are going to L-O-V-E it!"

Though you may be right—theologically, sociologically, and contextually—this is probably the quickest way to derail and stall all progress toward implementing even the best new initiative. Sadly, I learned this lesson the hard way.

I had been at my church for just a few years when I became absolutely convinced that one of the foundational challenges facing youth ministry was that almost every popular model fundamentally isolated teenagers from adults and from their families in particular. Scripture, research, and my own observations brought me to the conclusion that we had to start thinking about youth ministry in radically different, more intergenerational ways if we hoped to have teenagers leave our ministry with a faith that sticks.

So far, so good.

The problem came in how I managed my rightness. I started by making a series of pronouncements:

- To the students: "Next Sunday we'll be changing things. We're moving to an approach we call Family-Based Youth Ministry. We're going to make more time each week for your parents to be involved!"

- To the parents: "You have no idea how much power you have in the faith formation of your children. We'll be getting out of your way, and we're going to need more from you."

- To the leaders: "The way we've always done it isn't working anymore, and we're changing next week."

I neglected to bring it up to my senior pastor or my colleagues on the staff, but I figured that they would hear about the changes soon enough.

And I was sure right on that count.

Within a few weeks of implementing dramatically different program changes, I started receiving calls, my pastor started receiving calls, and my volunteer leaders started receiving calls. I met with most of the most highly concerned folks individually, and usually, after hours of explanation, I could get them to agree that I was right—at least the theory was right.

My pastor just wanted me to "take care of the problem" so that he could get on with his job and not have to worry about the uproar surrounding the youth ministry. These were tense days, a year or so when I considered relocation almost daily.

Then over lunch one day, a wise older friend met with me. Seeing my weariness, he asked lots of questions until finally, he made this observation: "So you're telling me that if you had just done Family-Based Youth Ministry and made a few gradual changes without talking about it so much, you wouldn't be in this mess. Is that right?"

He had me.

If I had slowly introduced changes, without making a big deal about them, I'm pretty confident people would have liked them. And when they did, I could have labeled them "Family-Based Youth Ministry," rather than overhauling the ministry so quickly that just about everybody (including me) suffered from a case of programmatic whiplash.

During that same season, I was visiting with the principal at my children's school, a brilliant leader. She introduced me to the phrase, "evolution, not revolution." Ever since, I've used that phrase as a guide to change management.

EVOLUTIONARY CHANGE MANAGEMENT

Let's apply the evolutionary approach to our what-if scenario about the convention epiphany.

Chances are good that parents, students, and volunteers are expecting the youth ministry to have a strong youth group on Wednesday night (or Sunday morning or whichever day of the week your group holds its primary meeting). If that component is not in place, you can expect to be crushed by a congregation experiencing the first four stages of grief— denial, anger, bargaining, and depression—and there's a good chance that the pressure around you will result in switching things back before your stakeholders reach the final stage, acceptance.

What would happen if, instead, you simply tried one first step in the direction you want to head, not announcing it as the "next big thing"? If it works, you would keep it and then try another step a few months later.

If the first step doesn't work (which is likely in any laboratory experiment), you assess what went wrong and try another step in the direction of the desired change. If this one works, keep it and add another one. A good trial balloon for small groups, for example, might be a six-week study at a popular leader's house. If all goes well, they'll be asking for another six weeks, and you'll deliver.

Once it looks like these experiments are gaining popularity, you can then begin rolling out an overall vision, meeting with key stakeholders and gate-keepers, and developing a clear game plan and timeline. Lastly—only after you have completed the process—go public with the plan.

It's as if you had a vegetable garden, but in your heart of hearts, you really loved flowers. Unfortunately, it's not just your plot of soil; you are the gardener for a community of folks who have been eating these vegetables for years.

If you take a rototiller to the garden and plow everything under, the village will be in an uproar and plant you headfirst in the freshly tilled soil. The better approach is to quietly plant a few flowers. Don't make a big deal of it. Just plant a few radiant flowers where people can see them.

When someone comes by and says, "Oooh, that smells nice," you smile and say, "You like that? I'll plant a few more for you."

Over the time, the right mix of vegetables and flowers will emerge, and perhaps most importantly, you'll still be there as the wise and beloved gardener.

MAKING THE MOST OF THE HONEYMOON

CHAPTER 21

Ashley's wedding is fixed in her mind as clearly as the pictures in her photo album. She can tell you the color of the tablecloth underneath her wedding cake, the songs played at her reception, even the names of almost everyone there. And although she can't remember everything they said, she knew she was beloved.

The honeymoon was everything she dreamed it would be—a whirl of excitement, chocolate-covered strawberries on her bedside, and a husband who told her she was beautiful 20 times a day. Wherever they went, people knew she was the bride and treated her like royalty.

Settling into marriage, though, was a different story. Soon, the reality of her post-honeymoon life began to pinch her like new shoes. She thought she had known all her husband's odd quirks, but he had dozens left to uncover. He had expectations of her; she had expectations of him. Most were met, but some generated unexpected frustration and disappointment.

In just a few short weeks, Ashley had gone from Princess of the Party to Queen of the Kitchen, and the new job didn't feel nearly as fun.

TO BE EXPECTED

If you have been in your youth ministry job for over a year, you may feel like the climate has changed dramatically—from a Caribbean cruise to Des Moines in December.

If you're there, you are right on schedule.

If you still happen to be in the honeymoon phase (or if you haven't actually started in our position yet), you can make the most of the honeymoon months. Here's how…

Start by taking a deep breath and reminding yourself (repeat after me), "It's not right, it's not wrong, it's just different." Reframe your role by thinking of yourself as an explorer discovering a new culture. Just like you might tell your students as they embark on a mission to Mexico, make a decision not to judge. Instead, seek to understand this strange, new territory.

Be prepared for the reality that your job (like any new job) will include a few unpleasant surprises. There will be things you were promised that will not materialize ("They said I'd at least have a desk when I arrived!"). And there will be other things that never came up in the interview ("I'm now the coach of the softball team?"). As each "surprise" comes your way, respond with non-anxious curiosity and good humor, rather than reacting as if every event were a personal offense.

START STRONG

You've likely heard the advice that you should not try anything new in your first year on the job.

Forget that advice.

If the church does not see some kind of return on its investment in the first six months, you may just be returning to section one of this book.

There is part of the conventional wisdom that is true, though. It's true that you won't want to dismantle everything that has been built before you showed up. Take time to figure out which events and customs are beloved and, for the time being, untouchable. If the lock-in is the biggest buzz-builder in the youth group, don't scratch it off the calendar this year, even if you hate staying up all night with middle school guys.

There will be a time for fighting that battle next year, after the parents and teenagers have fallen in love with you.

You can accomplish a lot without erasing beloved programs and traditions. There are plenty of things you can change that will cause the congregation to sing your praises.

LISTEN FIRST

It all starts with listening.

Listen to a wide variety of people who care about the youth ministry, and make a list of things the youth, parents, and leaders would like to change. Make another list of things you would like to change. Unless there's a glaring crisis somewhere, highlight the items that show up on both lists and start making immediate changes with those.

The key is not whether you will make changes in the first six months, but which ones and how. Many youth directors step in like a bull in a china shop and start knocking things over, offending and alienating students, parents, volunteers, and colleagues along the way. First make the changes that have the most consensus (for example, few people are going to be offended if you recruit more volunteers or get an accurate directory of youth in the church or communicate more regularly with parents). Make sure you have buy-in from your senior pastor and that he or she is fully apprised and supportive of the changes you are about to make.

When possible, develop a small team to help you develop the solution and implement it. You can probably make the change more quickly without a team, but the team creates a broader foundation for making the changes stick and provides a support system to help you troubleshoot the parts of the solution that just don't work.

When a victory is won, use all available media to praise the *team* that made it happen. By producing results and memorializing the win with stories, you will infuse the youth ministry with resilience and health.

As you creatively repair the broken places that your constituency cares about the most, you make deposits in the Respect Bank, deposits you'll need when you start tackling some of the more entrenched patterns you'll want to address soon.

SYNC ME

CHAPTER 22

Bekah knew a lot about youth ministry before she ever started in her part-time position on the youth team. She had grown up in a dynamic youth group. After college, she volunteered in her new church's program, and her job with a local social service organization put her in contact with most of her small town's youth pastors. And her extensive mission work in Thailand left her with a hard-earned understanding of how to minister to young women facing tough times.

In so many ways, she had earned the right to speak like an expert, to tell people how ministry should be done. But when she came to work at Christ Church, she invested months asking questions and listening. Every once in a while, she'd suggest a new idea, usually starting with the words, "Have you ever tried..." or "What do you think of...?"

We asked her about this humble strategy, and she said simply, "I'm still learning."

The church that hired her was larger than the one she'd grown up in, and its multi-staff structure was new to her. More importantly, it was a different denomination with different traditions and even a slightly different theological vocabulary. Bekah said her experiences as a missionary taught her the importance of studying a new culture, of not condemning things that seemed different, of learning before campaigning for change.

"In Thailand," she said, "I was ready to jump in and go, but I learned really quickly that there was so much I didn't know. To make the biggest impact, I had to posture myself as a learner, not a teacher."

BEYOND THE MISSION STATEMENT

Our job as youth workers is not to sell the church on *our* vision of youth ministry. Our job is to steward *the church's* vision. Even if that vision might feel fuzzy and fragmented at first, we need to care more about the church's agenda than our own (since there's a very strong chance that our particular church will be around longer than we are).

When someone in an interview tells you that you'll have "a blank slate," don't believe it for a second. Every church has a specific DNA, spoken or unspoken, written all over its "slate," even if it's written in old, faded ink.

You're in a blessed minority if your church already has a mission statement. You're even more blessed if that statement actually drives the church's behavior and offers you a framework for mapping out the youth ministry's future. But as you will soon learn, "it's not what hangs on the walls, it's what happens in the halls" that defines a church's mission. So start with the mission statement, but don't stop there. Keep learning.

WHERE IS THE MOMENTUM?

Your job will be a lot easier if you figure out which streams are already flowing and jump into those waters first. You will, of course, add your own unique flavor, but you'll be carried along by momentum you didn't have to create. To discover those areas, listen to the stories that the congregation tells. Where is the most energy? What is our church known for? What are the best-attended events of the year?

There will be plenty of time later for the harder work of introducing your congregation to parts of the Christian journey that may be missing. But you'll be wise to start with initiatives that fit the church's existing efforts.

HIDDEN VALUES

The mission and goals will tell you what the church is trying to accomplish. But its values can tell you more about the *way* it does life together. Again, a written statement of values (if the church has such a thing) would be the first place to start. But you'll want to observe what values actually get lived out.

For example, if the church names evangelism as a cornerstone value, but you see very few deliberate evangelistic efforts being made by the church, don't assume that everyone will be in 100 percent support of your inaugural Outreach Messy Night and Lock-In that attracts 90 percent unchurched teenagers. You might find out the value of evangelism is subordinate to the value of clean carpets, propriety, and taking care of our own students first.

This is not the time to try to correct or condemn the church for its inconsistency. You are first a learner. Only after you recognize and understand the *lived* values will you have the potential to help the congregation live into the values it aspires to and proclaims.

Part of becoming indispensable in your position involves learning the unspoken rules as well.

- "What drives the pastor nuts?" (being late to the staff meeting?)

- "What do people get praised for?" (staying in budget?)

- "What gets people in trouble?" (not telling the receptionist where they are?)

Your church hired you for your expertise in youth ministry, but you weren't hired to reject or denounce the church's culture or the direction it is headed. The church may have a DNA different from what you might have wished for. But the wise and indispensable youth pastors adjust their expectations and vision first to that of their churches. Ironically, when they do, they almost always are given a place at the table to determine their churches' future mission and DNA, and they make life exponentially easier on themselves.

WHEN NUMBERS COUNT

CHAPTER 23

Traci, a savvy youth pastor at a youth worker network gathering, said, "For me, it's not about numbers."

Traci is a magnetic and deeply spiritual person, a highly effective youth worker who after a decade in the same church has plenty of teenagers coming to her programs. No wonder the other youth workers around the table sit up and pay attention when she speaks.

The rookie youth workers are thinking, "Really? Oh thank goodness! I hate keeping up with numbers, and besides, our attendance is sliding. I needed someone to let me off the hook. Thanks, Traci."

But despite what is discussed around the youth ministry networking table, the truth is that those we serve (and those who have hired us) think about numbers differently.

Ask the students in a struggling youth ministry what bothers them about their youth ministry, as we often do, and you'll likely hear them say things like...

- "Nobody comes anymore."

- "All my friends are going to the church down the street."

- "It's just a handful of us in a big, fat room. It feels weird."

As much as we might hate to admit it, numbers play a role in how many of our students feel about our youth ministries.

When parents are evaluating our effectiveness, they say things like, "The numbers are dropping. What *does* our youth director do all week?"

And many senior pastors wonder things like, "I'm pretty sure we have fewer teenagers than last year, but maybe more than five years ago. I'm not sure because no one keeps close track. I know I hear complaints every now and then, and I don't know how to answer them accurately."

Don't kid yourself.

We can moan that "It's not about numbers!" from the top of the steeple, but it won't change reality.

So we do have a choice: We can be victims of the numbers or be their authors.

DEATH BY DIGITS

Numbers are not the enemy. Attendance figures help you decide how much money you should budget and whether you have enough volunteers. Target numbers help you buy enough ice cream but not too much. A consistent trend up or down is one of the legitimate measures of a ministry's ability to reach the flock God has assigned them—or to reach beyond the walls of the church to those not yet involved.

When you know key youth ministry numbers better than anyone else on staff, it will impact your credibility with church leadership. Compare these budget requests from two different ministries in the church:

The music ministry says, "Over the past 12 months, we have grown from an average of 31 to 45 choir members, and we need to purchase a dozen chairs at a cost of $120.50 each. We would like a one-time investment of $1,446 as well as an increase in our staff time by five hours a week to cover carry the added responsibility of more members."

And the youth pastor says, "We've got tons more students coming than we did last year. We really need more money to buy stuff for our programs. But the most important thing is that we need another full-time staff person because if we don't get one, I'm doing to burn out."

It doesn't take an MBA to know which request the keepers of the church checkbook will take seriously.

The landscape of youth ministry is littered with battered ex-youth pastors who were beat up with numbers. Death by digits.

But it doesn't have to be that way. When we track attendance and set reasonable participation targets for events, we actually have the chance to get people focused on the right figures. When the leaders of the congregation concentrate on the right figures, ironically, the anxiety over size and growth actually decreases.

HOW DO WE FIND THE RIGHT NUMBERS?

There are a few numbers we should totally ignore:

- How many students are going to First Awesome Church down the road?

- How many did we have in Sunday school in the Golden Days a decade ago?

- How many teenagers should we have coming on Sunday nights according to 50 different people's random, never-agreed-on opinions, discussed weekly in the parking lot?

But there are numbers, like the ones below, that faithful, indispensable youth workers not only know but also share with their church leaders:

- How many teenagers are in our flock?

- Based on this year's attendance and other trends, how many youth should we anticipate to participate in the coming year?

- How many high school students would we like to see participate in our summer mission trip?

- How many guests and missing-in-action students and families did we contact this week?

We need to kill the myth that bigger is better. Big numbers don't automatically mean a youth ministry is having a big impact on God's kingdom.

Clearer is better.

Little numbers don't guarantee a faithful ministry either. Quantity need not be the enemy of quality. As a faithful shepherd, you will, every now and then, need to count your sheep. In fact, you might not be able to run a faithful ministry without it.

WHY THE JONES MEMORIAL CARPET MATTERS

CHAPTER 24

The convention hall was filled with thousands of juiced-up youth workers hooting, hollering, and having a great time. The speaker was winsome and wise and hilarious. He captured beautifully the reality that youth ministry has a way of attracting a different breed of church worker. He painted a picture of the youth worker as a sanctified rebel, someone who, like Jesus, brings holy chaos to every endeavor.

"If there hasn't been a rule written at your church specifically because of something you have done, you're not trying hard enough!" he shouted. And the room went crazy.

During the break, youth pastors were in stitches as they regaled each other with their antics, each one outdoing the one before:

- "For some reason, the elders didn't *like* Frisbees in the sanctuary!"

- "Some of my students figured out the code for the security system and started having parties in the church attic on Friday nights!"

- "We've still got a hole in the Family Life Center exactly the size of Matt Richardson's backside"

They—OK, *we* were there sharing our stories, too—sounded a little too much like a gang of middle school guys huddled in the back of the bus, bragging about our bad behavior:

- "I drove my dad's car into the garage door."

- "My friends and I trashed our house when my parents were out of town, and they had a cow!"

...with each story followed by more explosive, uncontrollable laughter than the one before.

RESPECT BREEDS RESPECT

Youth pastors are right to insist that the church be sensitive to the unique culture of today's teenagers. But we often fail to apply that same cultural sensitivity to the generation that runs our church. We seem to expect the church to do most of the adjusting.

But consider this very real case study:

Let's say you leave the chairs scattered around the youth room and the markers spread out on the tables. For you, it's just life as usual. You'll clean it up tomorrow. To someone meeting in the same room the next morning, though, it sends a clear message of disrespect. You can argue that these folks need to get over themselves. But don't be surprised when you can't seem to get a seat at the grown-up table.

When a church leader reacts in frustration to one of our antics, we have a choice to make.

We can own the problem as ours and create a solution. Or we can respond defensively like a typical junior high student. ("What? I didn't do anything?" "You are *seriously* upset about *that*?!") We can own the fact that we created a problem for someone, or we can fixate on the less-than-loving reaction we received to little things (like broken water balloon pieces littering the lawn on a Sunday morning).

We want the church leadership to respect us when we have a budget request or a suggestion about the direction of the church, but we assume that we should just get a "Get Out of Jail Free" card when we fail to clean up our own messes. But the world doesn't work that way.

If we want our church to take youth ministry seriously, we'll need to take responsibility for taking seriously the things that matter to the others in our church family (as trivial as they may feel to us).

This doesn't mean that we should capitulate to the high anxiety of the least mature, most demanding complainers in the church. We can respond with love and own responsibility for our contribution to the conflict. We can apologize, make it right, and then initiate a process with the church leadership to develop *appropriate* policies for programs related to students. A well-written policy can provide a buffer between you and an unhappy member in your church. In this way, you do not have to be a victim of the policy; you can play a key role in drafting it.

INSIDERS ADVICE: WHAT BOB SAID

We asked Bob, a church administrator with lots of years of experience negotiating conflicts between youth workers and just about everybody, to offer his best survival tips for youth workers who want to cut off complaints before they ever happen. Here's what he told us.

"Tell everyone."

Let the congregation and church leadership know when you are about to do something edgy or potentially messy. Tell them in person when possible. The potential curmudgeons will feel honored, and you might just discover a few land mines before you step on them.

There is an old saying, "It's easier to ask for forgiveness than for permission." Easier?

Maybe in the short run, but it is unnecessarily time-consuming and potentially disastrous for your relationships with your colleagues in the long run.

Tell everyone as soon as something gets broken or goes wrong. Not tomorrow. Today. Tell them you did it and how you're going to fix it. Make sure you include the pastor in that communication loop. If you put a dent in the church van, your boss needs to hear it from you first. He'll want to speak calmly and knowledgeably if anyone complains, and he can only do that if he knows the full story.

"Know the difference between mess and damage."

"I don't mind mess," Bob said. "Tables can be cleaned, floors can be washed. But damage—holes in the wall, broken light fixtures?—that's disrespectful," he said. "You have to think, how would I feel if someone came to a party at my home and did that?"

"Recognize the holy ground."

When Moses was standing before the burning bush, he was told, "Take off your sandals, for the place where you are standing is holy ground."

What a gift it would be to teach our students that some places are holy—set apart—in honor of God. Discover those places in your church and honor them.

There is a valuable payoff that comes from treating church facilities well, cleaning up before you go home, and honoring sacred spaces. The payoff is indispensable trust and respect from the church, currency you'll need when (not if) you make your next major mistake.

CONGRATULATIONS, YOU'RE A POLITICIAN

CHAPTER 25

Like it or not, if you're a youth pastor, you're a politician.

Or at least you should be.

When people ask us for advice on how to "avoid church politics," they are usually asking something like this: "Can you help me just do my job without having to worry about complicated relationships with the difficult policymakers and stakeholders in my church?"

The simple short answer is no. The longer answer is that it's actually part of your job as a youth pastor to navigate those relationships,

It will basically be impossible for you to build a healthy, sustainable youth ministry if you isolate yourself and your ministry from the powerful decision makers in your church.

DON'T FIGHT; BE POLITE

When most people think of church politics, they somehow imagine sneaky, underhanded backroom deals made by powerbrokers with their own petty agendas. And though sadly, church politics can at times looks this way, we are convinced it is possible to "do politics" with integrity and to do it in a way that is actually a lot of fun.

It helps to understand politics in the purest sense of the word. If you flip open a dictionary, it will tell you that a politician is simply a person involved in influencing public policy and decision making. The successful youth pastor/politician is constantly making connections and finding the common ground to help move ministry initiatives forward.

If that idea makes you cringe, skip back a few words in your dictionary and you'll find the word "polite," which means to be civil and have regard for others. Investing in the habit of politeness is essentially what a good church politician does. Here's how it works:

In most churches, the authority to make decisions is spread out in a dozen different places. We might have a title that says we're "in charge" of the youth ministry, but the truth is that we have very little power that is not given to us both by those we lead and those with other responsibility in the church. That committee has to approve the budget, this person has to OK our calendar, and some board has to give a thumbs-up before we can throw away a torn-up couch. We can easily be surrounded by what author Jim Collins calls "a thousand points of no."[5]

If you don't have power, it's a bad idea to start a fight. You're bound to lose.

In youth ministry, we are called to exercise a more sophisticated kind of leadership that "relies more upon persuasion, political currency, and shared interests," to use Collins' words. So after we understand what each decision makers need in order to make an informed decision and how they like to communicate, it is our job to get them the information and experiences necessary to allow them to make a wise decision.

In each encounter, the polite thing to do is to listen for feedback, make corrections, and repeat the process until enough people are on board. Persuasion almost always takes longer than power, but the outcome is a more secure, sustainable ministry, one that will not be blown away as soon as you are gone.

UNDERSTAND FIRST

Janice decided early on in her tenure at Village Chapel that she was going to be particularly "polite" to her volunteer team. Her large team of volunteers brought a wide array of gifts as well as an even wider set of opinions on how things should be run. But Janice was able to nip potential battles in the bud by seeking to understand each person's perspective and listening first to everyone's concerns.

Instead of rushing in to correct her volunteers' attitudes and behavior, Janice took the time to listen and see things from many points of view. As a result, she avoided the kind of polarizing either/or thinking that is normal in so many churches. By working to appreciate each person's perspective, she could bend her own way of doing things, accommodating to her volunteers' preferences while still keeping the work from falling back into her lap.

After Janice retired, her replacement, Carissa, chose not to waste time "coddling" her volunteer team. She made it clear that she didn't have time for "playing politics." Soon, a conflict began brewing with two of the long-standing summer camp chaperones. They had their own ideas about how the trip should be run, but Carissa was not particularly interested in their point of view. She simply expected them to be "team players" and get with the program (her program).

She chose power over influence, speaking first, leaving listening to another day. She sent the message: "The church put me in charge, and I can't have two volunteers undermining my authority."

In the end, Carissa won the argument but wound up losing the chaperones three weeks before camp. She only found one willing soul who was old enough to drive the church van seven hours each way to drop the students off and come back a week later to pick them up. It was her senior pastor.

Though it may feel like the most natural thing in the world when tensions are high, focusing on "winning" is not usually helpful. Leading by power has a way of isolating us from the very people we need. Being a wise politician might not only save you time, but just might also keep you in the game of ministry years longer than those who go straight for the easy win.

THE END OF THE FIGHT CLUB

We church folk know enough about the Bible to over-spiritualize any argument. And sometimes, in a desperate effort to make ourselves feel less petty, we turn our opinions into black-and-white moral issues, often forcing Scripture to back us up.

If only we were battling for causes truly worthy of a holy warfare—poverty or addiction, domestic abuse or slavery. But sadly, 98 percent of the church battles we've seen—or been involved in—have been over things like budgets and paint swatches, schedules and drum sets.

At the same time, we've observed a number of ways to continue working toward change while sidestepping the resentment and damaged relationships that polarizing conflict almost always bring. Even before solutions are actually agreed on, this process has a way of helping people feel less trapped, less anxious.

RONNY'S STORY

Ronny was excited to land a job with a Christian organization right out of college. He looked forward to praying with his coworkers, bringing his Bible to work, and laboring with like-minded peers to save the world. His heart sank, though, when he discovered he was working with regular human beings with their own sets of sins and struggles.

He loved the ministry and had great respect for the skills of his coworkers, but the gossip and negativity were wearing him out. When he traced the cynicism and rumoring back to the manager of the organization, he felt trapped. He wanted to confront his boss, but he wondered if it would do any good. Would she listen, or would she just make his life miserable?

Based on the advice of friends, Ronny began to pray. An idea began to form.

He waited a few months, making friends and contributing to the ministry because he knew that his idea would require him to have credibility with the team.

One day at a staff meeting, he stuck his toe in the water.

"I love working here," he said. "And it's fun getting to know each person and watching the way we all serve Jesus together as a team. I think we're doing important work and doing it well."

He paused to muster up his courage.

"But has anyone else noticed that we sometimes have a problem with gossip and negativity?"

There. He'd said it. His game plan was to talk about the culture, rather than specific people. He thought that if he came alongside rather than attacking the group, his odds might improve. He included himself as part of the problem. And he asked a question, rather than making a statement. He was prepared for people to tell him that he was wrong, but he hoped they would agree.

"I know what you mean," said Amanda, who had been working there a while. "I feel it, too, sometimes. I think I even play along." And even the manager had to admit that she, too, had grown comfortable with the floating negativity that had become normal among the staff.

What followed was a healthy conversation about how team members would like to be, and they all agreed to work on protecting a more positive staff culture. They even created a few systems for holding one another accountable.

Ronny's approach allowed him to break out of his trap. He was clear without being confrontational or arrogant. He stayed connected without being enmeshed in the full-blown anxiousness of the staff culture. He asked curious questions rather than making accusations:

- What would happen if...?

- I may be missing something, but I wonder why...?

- Can you help me understand...?

- Is anyone else having this problem...?

DON'T FORGET THE WARNING LABEL

It worked for Ronny. But just because Ronny's brave experiment worked doesn't mean these kinds of conversations will always go smoothly for the rest of us. In fact, when you raise questions from a self-differentiated stance, things may get worse before they get better; you may raise anxiety before it is reduced.

But if you hope to change a negative culture around you, take a page out of Ronny's book and pray for the "nerve" simply to ask the risky questions—questions that might just launch the slow, sometimes-turbulent process that leads to lasting, systemic change.

HOW TO EARN
FREEDOM

CHAPTER 27

Raychelle has been doing youth ministry at the same church for more than a decade. She loves her church, and they love her.

Almost every week, someone who has very little connection to the youth ministry stops Raychelle in a store or in the church hallways and says, "We love what's going on in the youth ministry. Just keep doing what you're doing."

Usually she just smiles and says, "Thank you" or "God is good." But on one mischievous morning, she responded curiously, "I'm just wondering—what do you think we're doing in our youth ministry?"

After a long, uncomfortable pause, the startled church member said, "Well, actually, I have no idea, but from where I'm sitting, it sure seems to be working! Keep it up!"

Most people at your church don't know the details of your youth ministry, and they don't really want to (or even need to) know. They're focusing their attention on other parts of the church.

Rather than taking offense that not everyone in our churches is totally informed about our youth ministries (despite our scintillating newsletter articles), we can accept the great news that we don't have to keep *everyone* informed about *everything* in order for our congregation to be supportive. Typical church leaders grant us youth workers tremendous freedom to experiment and innovate, as long as they have a general sense that we're handling the basics well.

To help keep our congregations and church leadership excited about the youth ministry, there are a few bases we'll need to cover. We call this process "paying the rents."

Paying the rents of youth ministry involves meeting a few foundational expectations. Meeting these expectations is not the goal of the youth ministry, just like paying our rent check each month isn't the goal of having a home. Paying rents, though, does provide a starting point from which to build. Another way to say it is that paying the rents doesn't guarantee that we'll be running a healthy, faithful ministry. It just guarantees that most people will think we are and will grant us the freedom and support we need to build one.

Here are the three rents that we have seen produce the greatest impact in terms of providing youth workers with freedom to lead and innovate:

Rent #1: Numbers—A significant percentage of youth need to be participating visibly in some aspect of the church's ministry. Although youth ministry is about more than numbers, people always want to know "how many are coming?" Rather than let a hundred different people evaluate using a hundred different numbers, we can agree on target numbers with our church leadership and the youth team, understanding that it is a target, not a pass/fail test of the ministry.

Rent #2: Programs—In order to "earn the right" to experiment with changes, you will need to provide the church with a few visible, effective youth programs that give both students and parents "something to talk about." The ladies at Bridge Club and the elders on the golf course will likely be talking about the youth ministry at some point. Having something—some visible program—that seems to be working will keep those conversations on a positive, healthy track. The lack of visible, effective programs will naturally create a vacuum that can lead to a downward spiral of negativity.

Rent #3: Enthusiasm—The enthusiasm and positive attitude of the youth staff, volunteers, and the teenagers themselves are essential to building trust with the leadership of the church and with the parents.

The people who stop Raychelle in the halls mainly know that they see wonderful teenagers who seem excited about their church and their faith.

EXPERIENCE DOESN'T COVER THE RENT

Sadly, some experienced youth workers step into a new church and *forget* to pay these rents. They assume that because they have had success in the previous ministry, the church should not care about such shallow metrics as numbers, programs, and enthusiasm. As a result of avoiding their rent payments, these youth workers pay heavily in other ways—some being dogged on every side by criticism and others losing their jobs altogether.

Remember the power of memorializing your events for the congregation through stories and articles, sermon illustrations and website updates. Don't just "slip the check under the door." None of us got into ministry because we wanted to be PR directors. But you'll soon find that a little reporting and celebrating will save you time, and your friends in ministry will scratch their heads and wonder why you are so lucky to have a church that seems to always give you the green light.

Pay the rents, and almost always, your church will affirm what you're doing and give you lots of room to play. Become delinquent on your rent payments, and you may just find yourself micromanaged more than you would ever wanted to be.

TELL ME A
STORY

CHAPTER 28

Sixteen-year-old Amy is new to your church and delightfully new in her faith. One Sunday morning, she pulls you aside and says, "I keep hearing everyone saying the Lord's Prayer. I think I get most of it. But what in the world is God's kingdom?"

What do you think your answer might look like? Would you say something about the rule of an eternal sovereign God over all creatures or about God's desire to rescue and renew a world marred by sin? If you did, you would be accurate.

But if you asked Jesus, he'd take a different approach. He'd you a story.

"The kingdom of God is like a mustard seed," he'd say…

>…Or like a farmer sowing his seed.

>…Or like a hidden treasure.

>…Or like a mess of good fish and bad fish in the same net.

Jesus knew all things, yet he chose to talk about seeds and pearls. He had a way of knowing the big words yet using the small ones. He knew how stories engage hearts and minds in ways that lead to real learning and life change, enlivening complex concepts in ways that capture the imagination.

Tell someone your mission statement, and they will forget it before they get in the car. But tell them a story, and it just has a way of sticking.

You can tell people that your Bring-A-Real-Friend (BARF) night attracted 52 teenagers, and 10 of them were first-time guests. A few might remember.

Or you can say, "I wish you could have been there! The parking lot was packed. We had two huge yellow waterslides. Pastor Jerry took a dare from one of the new teenagers and went down the waterslide—twice! I seemed like one out of every five faces were new students. You know shy Jenny? She brought three friends from school, and two of them said they'll be back next week!"

Stories are not just a more interesting way to share important truths; they actually have the power to shape culture. The one who tells the stories is, in many ways, the one who shapes the future.

If the current stories about the youth ministry are mostly negative, designate yourself as the singer of new tales. Share your good news stories often and with as many people as you can. If the only youth articles going into your church newsletter are announcements and calendars, you may be missing the opportunity to shape the culture of your ministry, missing the chance for your youth ministry to become indispensable to the church. After all, 80 percent of the people in your church don't care when the retreat is, but they can all be inspired by a story of how God touched a teenager's heart that weekend.

Smart youth workers always have a pocket full of five or so stories they can tell at the drop of a hat. Each story has a hero, a challenge that had to be overcome, and usually an emotional kick. They always star someone other than the storyteller.

These stories get planted in the soil of the church, and they bear the predictable fruit of celebration, support, and enthusiasm. The stories that the youth pastor tells are the stories that get repeated. You can spin culture-shaping tales of hope, perseverance, and joy, or you can tell tales of frustration and disappointment. Just remember that whichever you choose, the stories you tell will likely shape the climate of your ministry's future.

Not everybody in my church is a youth ministry fanatic. A few are unhappy and most are indifferent. But I love to tell our congregation the stories of how much they love their teenagers. I love to let them know how blessed we are not just with our students but also with the adults in our church who treat our teenagers like family.

We get what we focus on.

If our stories focus on frustration and failure ("No volunteers are willing to do the lock in!"), we'll find the frustration multiplied. If our stories focus on transformation ("When this kid first walked in the door, we thought…"), life change just gets imbedded in our DNA.

We have a choice to make. We can struggle under the weight of a church mythology that was dropped on our shoulders, or we can be architects of the future. Go ahead. Tell me your story.

THE ART OF THE WOO: UP, DOWN, AND SIDEWAYS

CHAPTER 29

We made a huge change in our youth ministry's Sunday morning format a few years back. Things were going well, and teenagers liked what we were doing, but we had clearly hit a plateau, and if we weren't careful our very stable program would become a very stale program. Though the students who were coming were satisfied, we had all become way too comfortable with more than 200 of our teenagers staying away on most Sundays (not to mention those outside of the church that we might hope to reach).

It was clearly time for a little reinvention.

We assessed our situation and developed a well-considered rationale, along with a clear timeline and a detailed implementation plan. Our youth staff was totally united. The appropriate committees approved the plan. We explained our rationale to our volunteer leaders and even met individually with a few of our more resistant leaders, enough to ensure their silence if not their support.

And then we started to work our implementation plan.

But within six months, the new plan had launched, sputtered, and simply failed to get off the ground.

What had we missed? We had taken all the steps, hadn't we?

1. Assess the need

2. Identify the high-leverage change point

3. Develop a rationale

4. Create an implementation plan and timeline

5. Implement

6. Enjoy the victory

Our mistake, I now realize, came right between steps 3 and 4. I refer to it as a woo deficit. "The woo" is simply the process of bringing others on board with your vision. In our particular situation, people gave an affirmative nod, but they weren't really on board. "The woo" is about moving people beyond "OK." It's about building enthusiasm and momentum. If you don't have it, go back and do some more listening. What is preventing people from enthusiastically jumping on this train? Either you're missing something or they are. It's critical to figure out which. Impatience, like we displayed, will shoot you in the foot.

The more dramatic the change, the more essential the woo.

A woo deficit has the power to sabotage the most well-thought-out plan. It can turn all of our highly organized goal-accomplishment strategies into fairy tales of what might have been. A woo deficit is doubly dangerous because it is so invisible that it is almost always left off of the implementation timeline, just like it was with mine.

We learned the hard way that there are three kinds of woo required in launching any new initiative, three steps that should be inserted right between steps 3 and 4 above and continued until the plan has all the momentum it needs.

My first mistake was failing to "woo down." I failed to connect with enough students to get their buy-in to the changes *before* we made them. Instead we plowed ahead, wondering why our teenagers just weren't getting with the program like we'd hoped. As a result, by the time I got around to listening to them, the viral negativity had spread, with many of our group voting with their feet, certain that we simply didn't care about how these changes were affecting them.

Second, I failed to "woo sideways" with our volunteer leaders. Confronted by unhappy students (some of whom were their own children), these leaders tried to support the new plan, but eventually they grew weary of trying to explain a rationale that they didn't totally buy in the first place. Though it would have slowed down our progress and extended our timeline, it would have actually *saved* us time in the long run if we'd practiced the fine art of the woo with our leaders. One other aspect of wooing sideways was that the other pastors at the church were blindsided by parents', negative comments about the youth ministry, because we had done nothing to prepare them with a reasonable response.

The third and final woo is "wooing up," probably the most important woo of all. We got our senior pastor's approval (which he gave readily). But we needed to prepare him for the criticism that was certain to come when trying to move from "the good" people had grown comfortable with to "the great" they didn't yet know they wanted. Once complaints started arriving on his desk, he remained supportive but in a cautiously tentative, looking-over-his-shoulder kind of way. Our failure to woo up cost us, not just in the immediate situation but also by diminishing the confidence and trust of our senior leadership.

The art of the woo happens not just when we are launching new initiatives. We build trust with our colleagues when we do what we said we would do when we said we would do it. It is possible for us to architect the kind of support we will need when we have to make tough and unpopular decisions. There is nothing wrong with taking bold steps that move our ministries beyond their comfort with the status quo.

Just don't forget the woo.

THE DEAD-AIR DEATH TRAP

CHAPTER 30

Imagine you're a pilot 20 miles from the airport, starting to bring your twin-engine prop plane in for a landing. But something's not right. One of the engines is making unsettling noises, complemented by explosive bursts of fire from the exhaust.

From the cockpit, you call nervously to the tower. You need clearance to land quickly. Who knows. You may have only one shot. Your heart is racing as you speak the words, "Apple Niner Niner to tower. Apple Niner Niner to tower. Come in please."

You wait. The radio silence is deafening. Your blood pressure is rising. You try a different channel, an emergency frequency. You receive again nothing but dead air. It is becoming harder and harder to control your plane as it pitches to the left for unexplained reasons. You radio again, louder, this time with the mayday signal, alerting the tower that you have an emergency and need a response *now*. The silence creates in you a combination of terror and raw anger at the air traffic controller not at his post.

You promise yourself that if you make it down safely, you'll be giving somebody in that tower a piece of your mind. And you'll be quick to tell all your pilot friends never to trust the idiots in that tower again.

The way that you would feel as a pilot in that scenario—that's the way parents, volunteers, and your pastor feel when you don't respond to their calls and e-mails. When a parent or your pastor reaches the mayday mode, the damage you have done to your future freedom in your ministry at your church has been severely damaged.

I hope you hear this. You can lose your credibility with parents, colleagues, and your boss by doing *nothing*. You don't have to *do* something wrong to lose the trust of parents (and all the people they talk to); all you have to do is *not respond*. But sadly, that's exactly what otherwise very intelligent youth pastors do on a far-too-consistent basis. Take Jim, for example.

Jim was a busy youth pastor. A few times a week he would scan through his voice mails and his e-mails to see if there was anything he had to deal with immediately. It wasn't that Jim *decided* not to call back. And in fairness to Jim, he responded back most of the time.

But on an almost weekly basis, there were questions from parents, e-mails from volunteers, even voice mails from the boss that were left completely unanswered. Jim might argue, "Maybe one or two out of 10 calls get missed—that's not a bad percentage, is it?

In baseball, it's a superstar percentage. In trust building, it is unacceptable. If you want to lock in your youth ministry position, you'll have to do much better than Jim's average.

Here's how:

1. Make it your practice to respond to key calls (from colleagues, volunteers, parents, students, and your boss) within 24 hours and to their e-mails within 48 hours. There may be calls and e-mails from others that you can wait longer to respond to, but as much as possible, respond quickly to your key ministry contacts, even if the response is "I'm underwater right now getting ready for this retreat. Can I be back in touch with you on Monday?"

2. Never trust your memory. Write down the calls you need to make. Jim simply trusted his memory to remember to get back

to those who had contacted him. And once a week he would scan back through his saved messages to see what he'd missed. But every day that passed was one more day that the blood pressure of the anxious caller got higher. Remember, the dullest pencil is better than the sharpest memory.

3. Use your commute time (if it's legal in your state) to respond to the messages of the day. Remember, you don't have to talk with anyone voice to voice; they just need to hear back from you. Most of your callbacks will be voice mails, making it possible for you to make more calls than you might expect on your drive to and from work.

4. Handle your mistakes with humility. There is a world of difference between, "Would somebody around here please give me some slack? I missed a few phone calls? So fire me!" and "I'm so sorry it has taken me so long to get back to you." You don't have to be perfect, but the way you respond to your mistakes will determine the difference between a church that gives you trust and freedom to do your work and a church that micromanages your every move because its leaders don't know if you will drop the ball.

5. Capitalize on the miracle of texting. If you have multiple callers on your list who have texting on their phone, you can get back with a dozen or so of them in 10 minutes with a quick answer or texts setting up times for phone appointments. Texting comes in handy when you have lots of calls to return but don't have time for any one of them to turn into a long conversation.

There are few things that create instability beneath your ministry quite like giving radio silence to the people in your church who matter most— parents, leaders, students, your boss. In our assessments in quite a number of anxious youth ministries, one pattern we almost always hear is "I called the youth pastor to volunteer (or ask a question or tell about a problem or set an appointment), but I never heard back."

Silence is not always golden.

HOLY PARENT-O-PHOBE, BATMAN!

CHAPTER 31

Youth workers and parents are partners. And together, they have the potential to be a superhero team. But between the two, which one is the superhero and which one the sidekick?

Doug Fields reminds us that most of us youth workers act as if we see ourselves as Batman and parents as Robin (our sidekick helpers). Sadly, even more youth workers see themselves as the solo superhero—the Superman figure, with no sidekick at all—and see parents as the ones in need of rescue or simply as expendable townspeople who just get in the way.

We don't clearly understand youth ministry, though, until we recognize that the parents are the ones with the superpowers. We are *their* helpers.

Too many youth workers enter youth ministry as parent-o-phobes, fearful and distrustful of parents. But any youth worker who wants to "lock in" his or her youth ministry job will need to learn a few powerful practices of partnering with parents:

- Though it should go without saying, it all starts with acknowledging that parents *exist*. This process begins by our learning their names and building friendships with the parents of our youth, in much the same way we would build friendships with students. We can either be engagers of parents or avoiders of parents. We need to know parents and let them know that we are on their side *before* the crisis hits or discipline problem arises.

- When teenagers are at a pivot point in their lives, the parents need a call from the youth pastor. For example, before your new sixth- or seventh-graders step into youth group for the very first time, you can reduce a lot of anxiety for parents simply by introducing yourself and giving them some idea of what they can expect in the coming year.

- Every complaint from a parent gives you the opportunity to affirm your partnership and work collaboratively to come up with a solution to the parent's concern. Every complaint gives you the chance to write the "last great chapter." Your response will determine whether parents virally share their complaint or virally share their gratitude for your response. A defensive posture almost never works—in marriage, in your job, or in partnering with parents.

- Remember that your first job is not simply to get parents to get with *your* program. Your first goal is not to get them to come to parent meetings or to volunteer or even to understand the mission of the youth ministry. Your first goal with parents is to communicate that you are *for* them, that you are there to help them accomplish their mission with their children, not the other way around.

- You can earn a lot of "street cred" just by being polite— by responding quickly to parents' calls and e-mails, by communicating clearly about the timing and cost of upcoming programs, and by beginning and ending your meetings on time.

- When you have a teenager who has dropped out or is on your directory but never been involved, check in with the parents. A message like "We would sure love to see Jack become a part of the youth ministry. Would you have any recommendations on how we might best connect with him?" can go a long way, whether or not you are ever successful at getting Jack to come back to your youth ministry.

Parents can be one of your greatest resources for logistical support, volunteers, and sheer encouragement. Unfortunately, too many youth workers seem to work hard to keep parents *out* of youth ministry. It's like stepping on the garden hose and complaining that you have no water.

Here's the good news: The vast majority of the parents in your youth ministry desperately want you to succeed. They know that your success will make their life easier.

Here's the realistic news: Many youth workers *have* crashed and burned on the rocks of parental criticism. Though parents are technically not your bosses, responding inappropriately to their concerns *can* cause you to lose your job.

But you can be different.

Rather than being the victim of parents' perceptions, you have more power than you think to architect those perceptions. It all starts by recognizing (without blame) that all parents will evaluate your performance through the lens of their own sons and daughters. For an individual parent, the key factor is not what the numbers are or how many new students have become involved but whether their sons or daughters feel connected and *want* to come.

You don't have to be 100 percent successful, as long as parents know that you are giving a 100 percent effort at connecting with their teenagers.

Just remember who the real superhero is.

THEY ALL HAVE NAMES

CHAPTER 32

"What is your secret for learning people's names?"

"The secret," I say, "is to decide to learn people's names and work at it."

When we hear would-be youth workers say, "I'm just no good at names," we simply ask, "How much time did you actually spend in the last week *trying* to learn teenagers' names?"

Almost always, the problem is not some missing technique or some sort of genetic memory deficit. The problem is a lack of time actually devoted to the priority of learning the names of the youth and parents in our group.

Few accomplishments can help to solidify your ministry quite as predictably as learning all the names of the students in your ministry as quickly as possible. And nothing can create a fissure of instability beneath your ministry like consistently failing to learn students' names.

So if you hope to lock in this youth ministry position, you'll want to make it your goal that within the first month, you will learn all your students' names. If you happen to be in a church with hundreds of students, maybe you won't be able to have every teenager's name down cold in the first month. But shooting for it sure can't hurt.

Use a picture directory (or create one of your own with your cell phone camera), ask other students to help you, repeat students' names back to them when you meet them, keep notes on all the teenagers you meet. There are plenty of tricks you can use to learn names, but no trick works better than simply committing to learn names and taking the time it takes to actually do so.

IF YOU LIED IN THE INTERVIEW, DON'T BLAME THE CHURCH

CHAPTER 33

In the interview, Jacqueline seemed like the perfect fit for St. Michael's Church. She affirmed where the church was theologically, and she enthusiastically supported the direction of the youth ministry, which had been surprisingly steady for the past decade. When asked about her comfort with the church's style of music, she expressed unqualified openness to experience a new style of worship different from what she had grown up with.

Based on her years of experience in other youth ministries and her alignment with the vision of the church, Jacqueline was quickly offered the job in her final interviews with the pastor. The first few honeymoon months passed uneventfully, as she learned about the program, the volunteers, and the students.

Though Jacqueline soon developed close relationships with a handful of youth, after a few months, it was clear that something was not working.

Her subtle disagreements with the theology of the church, its "boring" worship style, and her dissatisfaction over her pastor's expectation of how many teenagers ought to be active in the youth ministry began to be shared quietly among trusted volunteers and student favorites. As the number of youth participating decreased, so did her resistance to the pastor's input, especially related to numbers.

It had been clear in her interviews that she was being hired not to overhaul the church's youth ministry but to steward its vision and maintain its healthy momentum. But within a year, most of the previous structure of the ministry had been dismantled in favor of a "model" built on the popular assumption that "what used to work in youth ministry doesn't work anymore."

Surprisingly, when long-term volunteers began to step down, Jacqueline was excited about being able to build a team of enlightened people more aligned with her vision. But sadly, she was the only person in the church she could find who was actually "aligned with her vision." Volunteers never came.

And the longer she stayed, the bitterer she became about the church and her situation. When, at her one-year evaluation, the numbers of youth participating had dropped to less than half the previous year, the concerns from church leadership became acute. When the pastor shared concerns about how many students had dropped out, Jacqueline more than hinted that if the worship style of the church were not so boring, more teenagers and families would be participating. After a long, emotional meeting with the senior pastor and the personnel committee chair, Jacqueline was put on a six-month probation.

Indignant about being so unfairly treated, Jacqueline was incensed that the church seemed to care so much about numbers and so little about theological integrity. She tried to convince the pastor that he simply didn't understand what real youth ministry was all about. She was not, she explained again and again, going to be about just flash and entertainment. She was going to do youth ministry "with integrity."

But could it be that Jacqueline's concerns had much less to do with theological integrity and well-nuanced strategy and more to do with the fact that she had been less than truthful in her interviews? She had assumed that once she got the position as youth director, she could (and, in fact, *should*) shape the position into something more informed and enlightened. And she was infuriated when the church had trouble seeing things her way.

Sadly, we've seen this pattern more than once: Candidates are willing to say just about anything to get a youth ministry job but then become resentful when the church expects them to be the kind of person they personified in their interviews.

There is nothing wrong with taking a job at a church that may not be a perfect match for you, particularly if other factors are in play—factors like being close to family or staying in the town where your spouse is already employed. We all know that there is no such thing as a perfect church.

What is wrong and absolutely hypocritical is to lead a church to believe that you will embrace its peculiar values and theology and structure and then do the exact opposite once you've been hired. In the long run, this approach only creates chaos and division in the church and defensiveness in you when the church holds you accountable to do what you were hired to do.

Remember, as a youth pastor, you are hired to steward the church's vision, not to undo it and import your own. *When* (not if) a youth pastor leaves (that would be you), the church will need a structure and strategy for ministry that is organic to the church, not something built off the latest youth ministry book. Too many ministries crater after the youth pastor leaves because that person is the lynchpin that holds the whole fragile structure together.

So if you want this to be a job that you'll be able to enjoy for a long, long time, go ahead and decide that you will not try to fix all the things that you said you'd be willing to live with when you interviewed—their stance on controversial issues, their overemphasis on fellowship, or their underemphasis on discipleship.

If you can make that decision, there's a good chance God will use you, imperfect as you are, in this very imperfect church.

WHEN YOU FEEL THE URGE TO FIX...

CHAPTER 34

If you think your church is messed up, you're probably right—not because your church is any more dysfunctional than the everyday, garden-variety congregation, but because it is, well, a church.

Gather a collection of broken people, all passionate about their own pet projects and priorities, all at various stages of self-awareness, and things are bound to get messy. Look at it this way: When you step into a hospital, you don't complain that there are sick people there. And when you become a part of a church staff, it is naïve to be surprised and complain about so many annoyingly unfinished people being on the ship you just boarded.

Though ideally you will be a contagious carrier of the DNA of God's kingdom, your job as a youth pastor is not to rescue your church from all its messiness and dysfunction. Your job is, in the very simplest terms, to do *your* job. In fact, if there is any hope at all that you *might* be an agent of healing and reformation in any church, it will come as you play the position you have been given well, rather than playing armchair quarterback for the rest of the church.

Of course, I didn't always feel this way.

When I first joined the staff of my church, I (along with those most excited about my coming) totally believed I could change the church—the one exclusively traditional in worship, pastors all in black (the color of joy) for weekly worship, parents with compartmentalized and nominal faith, and teenagers relegated to the basement, a space that doubled as an elementary school cafeteria.

There were so many things about the church I wanted to change as I looked down my disdainful nose at the mass of unenlightened members who desperately needed to move beyond their superficial understandings of God. (Translation: to become more *like me!*)

Now in my third decade at this same church, I've come to realize that God didn't call me, first and foremost, to "change my church" but to love it in all its peculiarity and brokenness. Maybe we youth pastors need to take a lesson in understanding the church from Augustine, the third-century saint who wisely said, "The church is a whore, but she's still my mother."

We misunderstand the nature of the church (and set ourselves up for grand disappointment) when we are surprised by its dysfunction. Sure, there will be glimmers of health in every church, but every faithful congregation I have ever seen is a mixed bag of the wandering lost and the comfortably found, of those who know they are broken and those who pretend they are not, of those who have staked their lives on the gospel and those who have made the church a fertile field to market their business and social enterprises.

Especially if you've had some success in your ministry, you will need to watch for creeping arrogance. We misunderstand ourselves and our own need for grace when we start to embrace the illusion that the church will be much better if it were just a little more like us.

On the flipside, I am convinced that healthy, long-term youth workers can, in some strange and mysterious way, make a difference in their churches. But we do so not because we are trying to get everyone to get with our program, but because we stumble faithfully alongside others in the church, each with a similar yet distinctly different sense of call.

The best we can hope for is to be midwives of the vision the Spirit is birthing in our churches. There are a few areas, though, that we can and must change, areas particularly related to our responsibility for the youth ministry. When you feel the urge to change your church, why not focus that energy on making these changes first:

- Change the fact that so few people volunteer in the youth ministry by taking the time required to work a volunteer recruitment and development plan (usually about two hours a week for six months should do it).

- Change the pattern of teenagers falling through the cracks because of a lack of follow-up by establishing the habit of making weekly updates to the youth ministry database, using the categories of member active, visitor active, member inactive, visitor inactive, first-timers, and students whose families have "changed churches." And work a process of staying connected in some way with all the students God has given you.

- Change the haphazard way that your youth ministry has done its planning by having your major events scheduled and published a year in advance.

- Change the disconnectedness between the youth ministry and the youth parents by learning their names, communicating clearly and regularly about youth ministry programs, and connecting personally with at least one parent every week.

- The list could go on, right?

Next time you hear yourself complaining about the church, ask yourself whether you're complaining about something you can change or something you really have no influence over. If it's in the second category, let it be. We can waste an awful lot of time worrying about things we have no power to fix.

PACING WITH YOUR PASTOR

CHAPTER 35

Pastor: How was youth group last night?

Youth Pastor: It was great. We had 40 first-time students!

Pastor: That's great. And how many total kids were there?

YP: *(doing a quick calculation)* About 45.

Pastor: *(his face shows disappointment)* So only five of our church kids were there?

YP: *(feelings hurt)* Yeah, most of your church kids just want to stay in their own little cliques. They don't really like having new students here.

Pastor: Let me see if I get this straight. We've got over 100 teenagers in our church, and only five are coming for youth group?

YP: *(getting irritated, feeling attacked and unappreciated)* Listen, I just work with the teenagers God brings me. I thought you'd be excited that we'd be reaching so many unchurched students.

Pastor: Sure, I am happy about that. What I'm concerned about is that I also want you to have a ministry that attracts and disciples our own teenagers. In fact, in the minds of many of our leaders, that's your first priority. We need to have more than five of our own students active in youth group.

YP: *(getting tense, with quivering lip)* So the church leadership wants me to babysit church kids? Sounds exactly like the kind of ministry Jesus had—keep all the religious people happy!? Yeah, that's a great idea.

Pastor: Are you really trying to make this about theology? I just want you to do what you were hired to do.

YP: What if what I was hired to do is unbiblical and self-serving?

Pastor: Working hard to connect with the kids in our church is unbiblical?

YP: *(standing to leave)* We just have a difference of opinion.

After a conversation very much like this one, my young youth pastor friend asked, "What do I do when the work I've been called to do as a youth pastor is different than what my pastor wants me to do?"

"Seems to me you've got three choices, but only one faithful response," I said: "You can...

1. Move to a church that will pay you to do exactly what you've been called to do, but until then, *do first* the top priorities of your pastor or supervisor

2. Stay, and *do first* the top priorities of your pastor or supervisor

3. Get a job doing something else that will support you while you volunteer to do the ministry that matters most to you—but until then, *do first* the priorities of your pastor or supervisor

Sound a little too one-sided? Here's my thinking:

On any team, there is only one head coach. As the youth pastor, you get to coach part of the team, but you're not the head coach. You can actually do great damage to teenagers, your church, and your ministry when you lead your part of the team in a different direction than the coach (even if your direction is a good and "biblical" one).

But I did give my friend a little wiggle room. I explained,

> *There are few professions that offer as much freedom to control our schedules like youth ministry does. As a result, if I am passionately*

committed to making my pastor's priorities my priorities; I will have plenty of time to do the things I feel uniquely called to do. Usually our pastors are not "against" us doing what we have been called to do; they are just "for" us giving our first attention to our pastors' priorities. The tug-of-war ends when we make the decision on the front end that our job will be to tend first to our boss' priorities before our own.

I had a friend who had a heart for inner-city teenagers and became frustrated with his "unbiblical" suburban church pastor who expected his youth worker to be spending his first hours reaching out to the youth of the church. Too many youth pastors I know over-spiritualize this kind of situation, demonizing their pastors for not being "biblical" enough.

But this conflict is not fundamentally a theological or biblical one; it is about responsibility. If I have a job a Starbucks, I am responsible to do my job "the Starbucks way," even if I have a heart to make coffee differently.

If you feel called by God to speak against or work against the vision of the church where you are serving, feel free. But quit your job first. That would be the most faithful and biblical thing to do.

I've heard some youth workers in conflict with their senior pastors paint themselves as being like John the Baptist or Isaiah. The prophets, these youth workers explain, regularly took their stand against faithless practices, particularly among those connected to religious institutions. But there is one major difference between the prophets and us: Isaiah and John were not being paid by the institutions they were attacking.

They were itinerant prophets; we are resident prophets. It is the height of hypocrisy to draw a paycheck from a ministry whose vision you no longer choose to support.

There will be times when we are called to speak a challenging word from God to our pastor or our congregation or our students. But to claim the theological higher ground and use it as a justification for not doing the job we were hired to do is a sure, unwinnable strategy.

You are destined for greater things.

HOW TO LOVE YOUR YOUTH MINISTRY JOB

———————— SECTION THREE ————————

You've been doing youth ministry for years now, your church loves you, and although no one is truly indispensable, your job is pretty safe. The process of becoming indispensable has been the focus of section two.

This third and final section answers a different question: "I know the church still wants me, but do I still want this job?"

Frustrations about the job's frantic pace cause us to ask, "How much longer can I do this?" Policies, programs, or even people that we've tolerated forever suddenly become too much to bear. And the vocational loneliness can be overwhelming. We can easily find ourselves short on time to build friendships with those outside our church but strong enough on boundaries to keep us from looking only to our parishioners to fulfill our need for life-giving adult friendship.

We've noticed, though, that many veteran youth workers defy the trend. After years at the same church, they continue to love their ministries. We've also discovered that staying fresh and energized in a long-term ministry assignment has less to do with the church where they're planted and everything to do with a resilient set of skills and attitudes that equip them to not just to endure their work, but to love it. These are the youth workers whose infectious joy and prevalent peace cause us to smile whenever we see them. After talking with dozens of veteran youth pastors who love their jobs, we've distilled a few of their secrets of longevity.

You've locked it in. It's now time to make this the job you'll never want to leave.

NO FRUIT—
NO FEAR

CHAPTER 36

I love this story that co-author Jeff tells on himself:

I live in Florida where gardening is supposed to be a cinch. Any doofus can grow things year-round in Florida, right?

OK...not every doofus.

I found out pretty quickly that every little shrub I planted had a way of mysteriously dying. So one afternoon in April, I came up with a brilliant idea: Give myself a slightly expensive gift of a big, healthy tree. I was sure that the problem was that I was just trying to be too cheap in my horticultural adventures. If I spent enough money, I assumed I could get a tree that wouldn't die.

"This is the one you want," Dennis, the owner of the local nursery, told me. "It's already 6 foot tall, 1.5-inch diameter. And a Golden Raintree is almost impossible to kill. You can completely ignore it, and this baby will grow to be 55 feet tall."

It was a serious investment, but it was worth it, or so I thought. I gave the tree lots of care and attention. I was rewarded with new green leaves, new branches. And a few months later, yellow flowers began to bloom, making it obvious how the Golden Raintree got its name. A few months later, beautiful pink pods began to appear, and I saw that it was good. I had finally redeemed myself as a gardener.

Just as I was ordering my new copy of Gardening Like a Pro*, the leaves turned dull and brown and began falling off one by one. I redoubled my efforts—fertilizing and pruning and talking nicely to the tree (hey, it was in the book). But soon there was nothing left to my arboreal trophy but a bare tangle of sticks.*

I took a picture of the pathetic tree and shoved it under the nose of the nursery owner.

"Some tree. I thought you said nothing could kill it!? What's up?" I was demanding a refund.

"Jeff," Dennis said, "You were born in Florida, weren't you?"

I nodded.

"Yep, I thought so. Let me tell you how it works in the most of the rest of the world—they have this thing called seasons."

I was quiet.

"Uh-huh," Dennis said. "Trees are supposed to lose their leaves in November. That's why we call it fall. It'll all come back in the spring." He smiled as he put his arm on my shoulder. "Try not to kill it in the meantime."

SEASONS OF MINISTRY

For the youth worker who's never experienced them, the seasons of youth ministry can come as a big shock.

Things are going along great. Your little garden of students is growing deeper and wider, when suddenly, out of the blue, something happens.

- Attendance drops

- You find yourself with half the volunteers you used to have

- Your budget is cut

- You're just not enjoying it like you used to

Our first instinct might be to find someone or something to blame. But you can save yourself a lot of stress if you start out knowing a little about seasons in your ministry. Sometimes it will be spring, full of blooming and beauty; sometimes it will be autumn, with the exhilarating harvest; and you can count on some hard, cold winters, too, when nothing seems to grow no matter what you do.

MAKING THE MOST OF WINTER

Youth workers who recognize the seasons can be content, even in the dormancy of the winter months. During the frosty times, take time to talk to a non-anxious veteran about what you're experiencing. He or she can remind you not to panic, can keep you praying, and can assure you that spring will come. You'll want to be sure to choose your fireside companion carefully. It is easy for those with less experience to try to immediately fix or overfertilize a situation that is merely seasonal.

Maybe the waning momentum you're experiencing is a hint that changes *do* need to be made. If the youth ministry has run a few years without a fresh initiative—if it's been coasting for a while—the winter season may be just the right time to gather the key stakeholders in the ministry and start dreaming again. If we want to keep our ministries fresh, we'll need to change the game in some way about every four to seven years. What got us here might not get us there.

A regular rising and falling seems to be God's rhythm for life. Youth workers who love their jobs learn to embrace the winter as a perfect time to accomplish all those things they couldn't get done in the wildness of spring and the harvesttime of fall:

- Spending quality time with volunteers and potential volunteers

- Dreaming with others about what God has in store next and developing plans to make it happen

- Shoring up the infrastructure: the directory, the calendar, the budget

When you commit to a climate of non-anxiousness, no matter what the season, you'll be liberated from the blame game and free to lead your volunteers, parents, teenagers, and colleagues through the fog.

THE GOLDEN RAINTREE UPDATE

It's been a couple decades now since Jeff's fateful trip to the nursery. And that Golden Raintree is huge—about the size of his house. But it *still* loses its leaves every fall.

MIRROR, MIRROR

CHAPTER 37

Everybody loves Rob. He has all sorts of things going for him: He's funny, smart, and when he looks you in the eye, you know without a doubt that he cares.

He delights in what's happening right now but still keeps an eye on the horizon for what's coming next. When there are 12 empty chairs in the room, people pick the one next to Rob. They know they will walk away just a little wiser and just a little happier than when they arrived.

Not that Rob is perfect. There are all sorts of things he can't do. But he has a "secret" weapon: He's great at recognizing the things he's not great at.

Rob knows how God wired him, and he's figured out how to make the most of the gifts he's been given. If you ask him, he can identify his weak spots with pinpoint accuracy. And he can point you to the people on his team who fill in the gaps in his gift set and the people who hold him accountable should he slip into easy excuses for not growing.

Most of the youth workers who love their ministries have made a regular practice of taking a serious look in the mirror. They can assess and describe what they see with clarity and honesty, free of puffed-up arrogance and paralyzing negativity. If you want to stay in the youth ministry game through the final inning—and still love it—it will happen because you choose to do things differently.

YOUR STRENGTHS

Someone might have told you once: "You can be anything you want to be, if you just try hard enough."

They lied.

You will probably never be an NBA® starter, a rock star, a nuclear physicist, or a thousand other things. You weren't designed to do those things. But that's not bad news. In fact, it frees you up to focus on the life you were created to live.

Understanding your strengths can tell you a lot about the kind of ministry you should be doing: whether you belong in the foreman's spot or on the front line; whether you should spend more time teaching, hanging out, or organizing things.

The key to great accomplishment is to invest time in your natural strengths. But as any football player, musician, or dancer will tell you, your potential doesn't become a real strength until you start practicing.

YOUR MOTIVATIONS

What drives you? Is it impact? freedom? guilt? affection?

Though often buried deep within us, our often-unknown motivations have a way of controlling our behavior. When we name what is motivating us, we can begin to make *conscious* decisions about which of these passions will be in the "driver's seat" and which ones will just be along for the ride.

Learning our hidden motivations is not a one-time event. It is an ongoing journey. And along that journey, we'll need to access different resources at different times. In one season we may need a faithful accountability partner; in another, we may need to battle our demons through disciplines of silence; and at other times, we will only move to a place of deeper understanding through a mentor or spiritual director. The key is to continue growing in self-awareness. Books, seminars, and personality tests can all be a part of the process. The particular tools may vary, but those who learn to *love* their ministries will be those who never stop taking a ruthless, honest, non-anxiously playful look at themselves.

The key, though, is not to use your new self-understanding as an excuse for bad behavior. It's helpful to learn, for example, that you are wired for relationships, not for organization. But if you stop there and say to your frustrated colleagues, "Hey, just get used to who I am!" you haven't done the world (or yourself) any favors. Just because it may not be your natural strength, you are still responsible to develop and hone the skills you will need in order to meet (and hopefully exceed) the expectations of your job.

YOUR HEART

The deep sadness we have observed the most in youth workers is a deep sense of vocational loneliness. It seems strange, doesn't it, for outgoing, energetic youth worker to express loneliness, but with deeper reflection, it only makes sense.

With most of our relational initiative being invested in teenagers and their leaders, it is only natural that we might have little relational energy to invest in relationships that feed our own souls. For some youth workers, their best friends turn out to be the students they work with— probably not the best strategy either for the health of the youth pastor or for his or her students.

Those who have learned to love their ministries are typically those who periodically step away from the rushing current of their work and take the time (they don't have) to build deliberate friendships with mentors and spiritual directors, with colleagues inside and friendships outside the church.

YOUR WEAKNESSES AND YOUR TEAM

Youth workers who try to embody every gift under the sun will soon disappoint themselves and everyone around them. I know I am not great at organization, so I work at it. I read books; I learn from organized, highly productive folks; I try to practice habits that don't come natural to me.

But no matter how hard I work, organization will *never* come naturally to me.

But I don't have to become an expert in all my weak areas. I just need to become proficient.

In my case, I try to surround myself with people who inhale and exhale order. I get to do the things I love to do and get to do those things with intuitive joy, and I get to have people in my life—some volunteers, some on staff—who make our whole team look better.

Leighton Ford said, "God loves us just the way we are, but he loves us too much to leave us that way." Long-term youth workers who love their work have discovered there's no shame in living like this reality really is true.

MAKE IT EASY ON YOURSELF

Robin knew all of the students and their parents. She was at every recital and every football game. She was a great listener, and her phone was on 24/7. She wrote her own curriculum and was great at designing snappy flyers. Without fail, she wrote a weekly newsletter, and it was rumored that she had once turned water into Gatorade®.

Teenagers thought she was awesome, the pastor called her a godsend, and parents bragged to their friends about "our amazing Robin."

Then, out of the blue, Robin quit.

She confided to a few friends that the ministry had felt like a burden for a long time, and frankly, the job of being a youth ministry superstar was killing her. When Robin decided she needed room in her life to meet a guy, fall in love, and get married, she couldn't figure out how to do those things while she was working at Good Shepherd Church. So she threw in the towel and never worked in youth ministry again.

THERE'S A BETTER WAY

Youth ministry is a lot of work. But it doesn't have to be a burden. Most of the master youth workers we know are not complaining about their work schedules or about how few volunteers they have. Instead, they tend to live at a much more sustainable pace because they have invested in the very unglamorous work of creating sustainable systems beneath their ministries. Building systems doesn't have to be mysterious or abstract. It can be as straightforward as the process we call "squaring the corners."

Squaring the corners starts with making sure your ministry has a few basic documents in place. They're not that exciting or original, but they are essential to building a youth ministry that is both anxiety-free and highly effective. Here they are:

- **Directories:** This is an easily accessible, annually updated database of all youth and volunteers who have ever been a part of your ministry. Each year, you'll want to distribute (at least to your volunteers) a printed directory of all active teenagers. For us, "active" teenagers are the ones who are members of our church and have attended at least once in the past year, plus visitors who have become a regular part of the group. You will also want a directory of all your current volunteers.

  In addition to your Member Active (MA) and your Visitor Active (VA) youth, you will also want to create a few other directories that allow you to follow up appropriately with different kinds of teenagers:

  - Member Inactive (MIA) Teenagers are still a part of the flock. You may not need to send them a Facebook message every time the group gets together for dodgeball, but you'll want to regularly pursue these students in some way, whether they ever show up or not. It's unlikely you'll pursue them without a plan. And it's unlikely that you'll work the plan without an MIA directory.

  - Visitor Inactive Teenagers are the ones who may have visited, but whom you are confident will never become a regular part of the group. This group requires no follow-up. But you'll want to keep their information in your system for that big event to which you'll want to invite everyone you know.

- First-Timer Teenagers are those who have visited. They aren't active enough to become Visitor Active (in the active directory) but have come enough that you are not ready to put them in the Visitor Inactive pile. This is the group you'll want to direct the most follow-up toward.

Without a well-structured database, you—like the vast majority of youth workers we know—will ignore tending to your directory for years on end, until in frustration every five years or so, you "purge" the rolls, removing a good number of students who might be ready to re-engage in your ministry. More importantly, you will, through your neglect of this very tedious process, ignore the very teenagers who just might need your ministry the most.

- **Annual calendar:** Stress-free youth workers already know in August what they are doing in April next year. Taking the time to build a 12-month major event calendar—and sharing it with the church—makes it easier to get parents on board, avoid schedule conflicts with colleagues, and recruit volunteers who can take much of the logistics weight of those events off your shoulders.

- **Job descriptions:** Without clear and regularly updated job descriptions, youth ministry volunteer roles will naturally devolve into one of three not-particularly-helpful types:

  - **Superstars** whose volunteer jobs expand to an unreasonably high number of hours. These folks receive much praise from the church, often serving as "the glue" that holds a ministry together. But not surprisingly, they tend either to be short-term volunteers (due to exhaustion), or they can cling pathologically to their position, preventing others from serving, all the while playing the martyr because no one is helping them.

  - **Burnouts** who used to be Superstars or were expected to be Superstars. This group generally wants to stay as far away from youth ministry as possible because they know how consuming it can be.

- **Little Helpers** who are willing to do little jobs, like being a "cookie mom" once a month. These volunteers may be recovering Burnouts, willing to do something but careful not to get too involved.

Well-defined job descriptions have a way of helping your volunteers be accountable for what they will do. But even more importantly, it stewards the investment of their time by clarifying what they will not be expected to do. Volunteers who carry a reasonable load for your youth ministry are the ones most likely to become fruitful and fulfilled volunteers who are ready to step up to the plate again.

- **Web of support:** Successful youth workers not only recognize that they need a team, they also invest about a third of their time wooing, recruiting, and developing their volunteers. All that hard work upfront results in a web of youth leaders who are highly invested in the program and in the teenagers. They allow the youth director to expand his or her impact without expanding the workweek. At times, these volunteers can even carry the ministry for a while when the youth director needs to rest.

A Master Recruiting List is the first step in building a web of adults who share the role of nurturing your youth. It contains each major volunteer opportunity you have for the year and how many you need (for example, "High school small group leader – 4; Ski retreat coordinator – 1").

Though you may not know it yet, you are already surrounded by the very people who care about teenagers and long to see your church build a deep-impact youth ministry. Tap into the most connected people, and ask for their recommendations. ("Who do you know in our church who might have gifts for working with teenagers?") Make a list of people you'd love to have on the team—about three times as many as you need. Match the names on your potential list to the blanks on your needs list and start making personal asks. Keep knocking until you find all you need.

- **A clear direction:** A clear vision and a set of written three-year goals can transform the atmosphere in a youth ministry. They free the ministry to focus on the most important things and give the team permission to put the latest "great idea" from anxious parents on the back burner. The same benefit is generated by a six- or seven-year curriculum plan that identifies what general topics are important to the church and how often they will be taught.

Most youth workers find that they need a little expert help developing the vision, goals, and curriculum plan, but the clarity and consensus are worth the hard work. It takes a lot less effort to move forward when everyone is rowing in the same direction.

THE REST OF THE STORY

After an exhausted and resentful Robin left her church, Good Shepherd hired a guy named Jim. He had big shoes to fill, and at first, people were concerned that he was not nearly as omnipresent as Robin had been. But he spent time in his first year not just working in the ministry; he worked on the ministry by squaring the corners before he got busy building.

Three years later, he's still a happy guy. One of the first things he equipped his church to do was to build a solid infrastructure. Working fewer hours than Robin ever did, Jim and his team are actually reaching more teenagers and parents. Going deeper, too.

Make it easy on yourself, but first be willing to make it a little harder on yourself by squaring your corners before you build.

LOVE THEM
ANYWAY

CHAPTER 39

Sarah had a favorite saying: "Love makes all the difference."

She ended every e-mail or voice mail with those five words. It was on her car bumper and on a bright yellow poster in her office. It seemed to be emblazoned everywhere—everywhere, it seemed, but on her heart.

When she was hired as music minister at Calvary Church, the staff quickly learned to tiptoe around the anger and resentment that she seemed to carry like a wounded lion.

When Nikki, the youth pastor, foolishly said in front of some church leaders that the new music style would "take some getting used to," Sarah went to the pastor and demanded that Nikki be fired. Nikki kept her job, but the incident taught her a few things: Watch your words, avoid Sarah whenever possible, and do ministry without her whenever you can.

To state the obvious: There are people in every church who are hard to work with. Quitting your job and running away from them is not much of a solution because your next church will have its own collection of alpha dogs, rebellious students, insecure parents, and territorial coworkers.

Youth pastors who love their jobs have adjusted to the fact that they bring their own brand of brokenness to their position, and that they, as much as any person they work with, desperately need grace. They embrace the fact that the church—even its staff—is not a collection of completed saints, but a collection of unfinished people working with other unfinished people. They have learned a kind of durable love—not an adolescent last-night-of-camp kind of love—but the kind that loves even when the ones we're loving make us work at it.

WHERE IT STARTS

Remember, no one can *make* us mad (or hurt or frustrated or…). Healthy, self-differentiated adults are not reactors. As one of our friends says about emotionally healthy people, "They let other people's stuff be other people's stuff."

When you are working with a chronically anxious person, your natural responses are, of course, fight or flight. But both are reactions through which we allow our behavior to be controlled by someone else's chronic anxiousness. Rather than running away or yielding to hair-trigger anger, we have a third, harder option: staying present in love.

Often a difficult colleague or church member is used to (and has become intoxicated by) people reacting to his or her aggression or passive-aggressive martyrdom. As a result, typical techniques for behavior management tend to be thwarted by these sorts of people. But those who take their focus away from fixing or punishing the behavior of difficult colleagues often have the greatest chance of seeing that negative behavior change. But it often gets worse before it gets better.

A LESSON FROM THE DOJO

The central principle for the martial art of judo—translated as "the gentle way"—involves using your attacker's weight and momentum to your advantage. We've seen it work time and again in ministry.

If a high-energy person, for example, cares enough to nose around in the youth ministry, it's often possible to develop a strategic partnership that ends up benefiting the youth ministry:

- Jonathan, the trustee who wanted to know why there were scuff marks on the floor, shared a lunch with the youth pastor and before long, became an advocate for repainting the youth room

- Margaret, who complained that there weren't enough activities, now organizes the egg-stuffer event every Easter

- And Molly, who complained that the teenagers ought to have a solid meal at youth group, now cooks twice a month

But that approach didn't work for Nikki.

STAYING IN THE GAME

Nikki worked hard to "get Sarah on her team," but Sarah stonewalled her at every turn. But Nikki was unwilling to hide from Sarah. Nikki neither cowered in fear nor reacted with eye rolls and anger. And by doing so, she upset Sarah's apple cart.

Sarah was simply not used to people not reacting and it made her behavior all the more erratic and anxiety-driven. Let's just say that staff meetings weren't always the most comfortable place for the two of them to be together.

With the help of a counselor, Nikki "differentiated" herself, recognizing that Sarah's reactivity was not about Nikki, but about Sarah. Nikki, like all of us, was used to being liked and appreciated. And it was not easy for her during those times when it was clear that Sarah despised her. As Nikki stayed healthy and present, Sarah's reactivity actually escalated, with snide comments to the pastor, random youth leaders, and even students.

Though the pastor could have stepped in and let Sarah know that her divisive behavior could not be tolerated, he withdrew into his office, wishing that Sarah and Nikki would just get along. Despite the chronic anxiousness of the entire staff culture, and even when there were tough conversations to be had over shared space, Nikki refused to resort to running away or attacking. She stayed in the game—present in love.

When the rich man came to Jesus, asking his arrogant questions about inheriting eternal life, Scripture says this: *Looking at the man, Jesus felt genuine love for him (Mark 10:21).* Those words became the context for all the rest of their quite difficult conversation. Jesus gave hard answers, but he did it with grace and integrity.

EPILOGUE

It took three years, but Nikki was astonished to look up one day and realize that she and Sarah were enjoying the same collegial relationship that Nikki shared with other staff members. In fact, one day Sarah asked Nikki to lunch. As they were about to leave, Sarah actually apologized for the way things had started off between them.

"I had a lot going on back then, and I wasn't very kind. I'm glad you never stopped trying," Sarah said.

Nikki followed with her own apologies.

"And now that we've said it out loud," said Sarah, "let's never talk about it again."

It turns out that love does make all the difference.

NOT EVERYONE IS A YOUTH WORKER

CHAPTER 40

Imagine…

…a column by Billy Graham, complaining about Mother Teresa's lack of evangelism skills.

…or a letter from Rob Bell whining about the lack of time Shane Claiborne spends studying Hebrew.

Not likely, right?

Sadly, that same grace is found less often in youth workers.

Stop by any youth ministry convention, and you'll hear a long line of youth workers complaining:

- "The youth ministry is the redheaded stepchild of the church. We just can't get any volunteers."

- "Half of our church has never even come downstairs to see how we painted the youth room. They couldn't care less about you until your hair turns gray."

Across the room, though, youth workers who love their jobs are telling a different story. Marriba is saying, "I can't believe how good my church has been to our students. The men's group just started this homeless ministry, and they were thrilled when I asked if teenagers could join them." Chris is talking about the ladies who baked cookies for their lock-in: "The blue hairs—now, their chocolate chip cookies are legit!"

Here's the crazy thing. These two different kinds of youth workers come from almost identical churches: the same number of volunteers, the same funding. But there is a huge difference.

Chris and Marriba have learned to appreciate the wide variety of faithful priorities that people in their churches have. Rather than desperately trying to plug square pegs into the round holes of their youth ministry, they have given people room to express their God-given talents and passions in whatever ministry suits them best.

There is a joy-robbing arrogance that comes with asking, "Don't they understand how important we are down here?" Youth workers who delight in their churches realize they are not the "discarded" and "ignored." They are simply one *part* of the body.

We obviously believe our ministries with teenagers should be a top priority for the church. But we're not alone. Ask the quilters, the food pantry workers, and the worship leaders—most of them would say the same thing about their ministry area...and should!

WE'VE DONE THE MATH

We'll all be much happier when we realize that 95 percent of our church is supposed to be doing hands-on work in *something other than youth ministry*.

For example, in a church with 400 people in attendance each Sunday, you would expect about 40 active teenagers each week (10 percent is a good rule of thumb). In order to minister well to 40 youth, you need a ratio of about 1 adult for every 5 students—or eight adults each week. Let's triple that number to include plenty of volunteers to help out with special events throughout the year. That means you need about 24 or so volunteer leaders this year—leaving 376 people in your congregation who can focus on other ministries. The fact that most of those 376 never make it down to the youth room is actually not a problem. It's on target.

YOU DON'T HAVE TO BE A PLAYER TO BE A FAN

Not everyone needs to be working with teenagers, but that doesn't mean we can't build a huge fan base for our students. These are the church members who have other frontline duties outside of your ministry, but they are supportive friends of the youth and the youth ministry nevertheless.

Doug Fields, in *Purpose Driven Youth Ministry*, says we ought to work toward developing three different types of fans:[6]

- The Cheerleading Team, who "just shower us with confidence and support"

- The Resource Team, who "share their possessions or specialized abilities"

- The Prayer Team, who, you know, pray

Keep in mind that it's not *their* job to become fans of the youth ministry. It's our job to woo them and keep them informed and connected. Often some of our greatest volunteers came from those who were first our "fans" from a distance.

WHEN FANS ARE FEW

We love the advice Peter Bohler gave to John Wesley, founder of Methodism, when he was struggling mightily early in his ministry: "Preach faith until you have it, then because you have it, you will preach it."

In the same way, you can start telling stories about the way your church supports its youth until more and more members of the congregation live into that reality. Put those stories in the bulletin and newsletter. Share them at church leadership meetings. Then, as more and more catch the vision in moments of connection with students, start telling the new stories as well.

So what if 95 percent of the people in your church are apathetic about youth ministry? You don't have time to tell the stories of their apathy anyway. The stories you tell will be the stories that will be repeated. The stories that get repeated will define, in many ways, the future fan base of the youth ministry.

So whether you're at a convention, with your volunteers, or with your students, if you want to really love your ministry, focus on the stories you want to see multiplied, not the ones you don't.

A LESSON FROM
THE IMPROV

CHAPTER 41

"Always say yes."

Malcolm Gladwell, in his book *Blink* identifies those three words as one of the first rules of "improv comedy."

It might seem contradictory that an art form as free-flowing as improv would even have rules. But it does, and one of the most important is "always say yes."

"Bad improvisers block action...Good improvisers develop action," Gladwell writes.

Here's how it plays out: Each actor takes whatever is thrown at him or her. If the first performer says you're a deaf policeman on a unicycle, then that's what you are. If you say no, then you've killed the momentum. The rest of the team has no place to go.

Gladwell sums it up: "In the first case, the scene comes to a premature end. In the second case, the scene is full of possibility."[7]

Jeff happened to be reading *Blink* in 2008, right about the time the economy was tumbling freefall over the cliff. Like a lot of congregations, his church instituted an immediate hiring freeze.

Since the only open position was in the youth department, it felt like the teenagers were the ones designated to carry the full load of the church's economic woes. Jeff was pretty frustrated and spent a couple days in a snit over the unfairness of it all. He was ready to gather support for a fight to get those dollars back. His righteous indignation was so great that he was almost willing to call a halt to progress of his youth ministry so he could divert his first energies to this undeniably just battle. Almost.

Fortunately, before he could poison the rest of the volunteers and families with his toxic frustration, he read Gladwell's advice from the improv: "Always say yes."

His youth leadership team gathered together later that week and talked about the challenge facing the church—and the youth ministry. They agreed that in this season especially, their stance would be to say yes, trusting that God was not overwhelmed and surprised by this challenge in the least. Jeff says that once he moved out of the "no" posture, the story was free to continue and ministry continued to happen. About 18 months later, the position was fully reinstated, and it felt like a great gift.

When unexpected changes come your way, just pretend you're part of an improv comedy troupe (not a bad metaphor for ministry, actually). Deadly seriousness, defensiveness, and launching into polarizing the church have a way of stopping the story in its tracks and slowing down your progress toward building the ministry you want. Youth workers who love their jobs aren't surprised by the unexpected, out-of-left-field kinds of interruptions that stymie most people. They say things like…

"Sure, I need a little advice"

A year or so into my ministry in Nashville, we came to a conflict over space with another ministry of the church. The traditional space where the youth met for youth group, "The Pit," was being taken over by the burgeoning office needs of our church's recreation department and its basketball leagues, soccer leagues, and other programs.

I went to our senior pastor and said, "We don't have a space to meet for youth group."

My pastor said, "What's wrong with The Pit?"

"It has now become offices for the rec department."

I got a great reaction! My senior pastor was indignant. At the next staff meeting, he confronted the recreation director, Bill, one of the wisest men in ministry I have ever known. The pastor told him, in no uncertain terms, that The Pit was the meeting space of the youth and that the rec offices would need to be moved somewhere else. I tried not to smirk.

Bill responded with an easy yes. He said something like, "I totally understand," and asked the pastor, "After staff meeting today, could we walk down the hall and talk through where the best place might be to put those offices?" The pastor agreed, and the meeting ended uneventfully.

We never moved back to The Pit again for youth group. When the rec director and the pastor went down the hall, it was clear that there really was no other option for the rec offices. Bill's ready yes made that reality quickly clear.

"Yes, thank you"

Three or four years into our ministry, we still didn't have a place for our youth to call home. (See the previous story!) After no little wrangling, we had worked out a reasonable plan for sprucing up a large closet at the end of the fellowship hall. It was not an ideal space, but there was room for a good number of students, and I was getting pretty excited about the idea.

Then my pastor dropped the bomb. "I've afraid you can't have the big closet we've been talking about." I was on the verge of being incensed (and unafraid of letting my feelings show). But over my emotional protests, my pastor explained to me that he had arranged for us to get a different space. Despite the fact that the new space was larger, better equipped, and had five times more storage than the fellowship hall closet, I continued in my resistance: "After all the planning we've done, I can't believe the church is trying to pull the rug out from under us *again*!" (Yes, maturity has always been a strong point of mine.)

But all my resistance only slowed things down. Within months we had moved into the space the pastor had arranged for us, and it turned out to be a coveted gathering space for our teenagers for the next decade.

I could have saved us all a lot of trouble simply by saying, "Yes, thank you."

EMBRACING THE CHAOS

It took awhile for our friend Karen to embrace this truth. In fact, it took her nearly two years at her new church before she fell in love with the teenagers there (OK, before she even liked them). Why?

Her heart was so invested in what she was missing—the students she'd just left at the old church, the church that had fired her—that she couldn't fully say yes to the teenagers who were right in front of her. Those trips down melancholy lane didn't help Karen or the students she'd left, and they certainly didn't help the teenagers in her new flock. There's a reason why the windshield in the front of the car is about a hundred times bigger than the rearview mirror.

Sometimes big changes in front of us force us to make an appropriate, though uncomfortable, shift in where we have been placing our faith: in a program, in a volunteer, in our own skills. An unsettling change can decenter us and remind us who our source really is.

I have a little beatitude that I use on days when I'm tempted to ignore the valuable lesson from improv troupes. It goes like this: "Blessed are the overwhelmed, for they shall be free of the shallow illusion of control." Saying yes frees us to love our ministries with all their unpredictability and to trust that no amount of chaos removes God from the equation.

FAREWELL, EEYORE

CHAPTER 42

The leaders at Trinity Church invited us to help their youth ministry develop a clear vision for the future and a concrete set of steps to reach their goals. It became quickly obvious, though, that nothing new could be built until we dealt with the toxic, negative environment we encountered at every turn.

The sense of helplessness and handwringing was a constant theme among parents and volunteers:

- "Nobody really wants to be here anymore."

- "The youth group always gets the leftovers."

- "No one even knows what's going on at this end of the building."

- "The pastor has never darkened our door."

- "We are on the ragged edge of exhaustion, and nobody even cares."

Their comments caught us off guard because in so many ways, this ministry was seeing results that churches all over America wished they could claim. Where was all the negativity coming from?

We soon found out. It was coming from the top of the youth ministry.

When we talked to Marcus, the youth pastor, we heard all the same sentiments—sometimes the exact same words—come out of his mouth.

It was part of his shtick—a role he'd probably played for most of his life. Some folks love to be the cynic in the room (Marcus preferred to call himself the "realist"). When someone says, "The picnic was loads of fun!" Marcus was always quick to add something like, "Maybe next time more than three parents will show up."

It was becoming clear why it was so hard for this ministry to keep volunteers and to woo others to invest in the ministry.

Remember Eeyore, the sad, gray donkey from the Winnie the Pooh books and movies? On the map of the Hundred Acre Wood, his home is tagged "Eeyore's Gloomy Place: Rather Boggy and Sad." He has a low, somber voice and says things like, "It's my birthday, and nobody cares."

He's loveable, but he's not much of a leader. Sadly, we've seen too many ministries run by an Eeyore. If you want to love your youth ministry job and if you want to attract people who stay, it may just be time to say farewell to your inner Eeyore.

USE THE EEYOROMETER

Before you try any new initiatives or plan for the future, do an environmental checkup. Are people telling positive stories? Are they excited about what God is doing in your youth ministry? If not, commit to telling new stories and creating a new climate before you try any glitzy new programs or switch to the latest, super cool curriculum. It's fruitless to plant something new in frozen soil.

SWITCH OUT OF VICTIM MODE

You can be absolutely certain that you'll face some hard days in youth ministry. Letting go of your inner Eeyore doesn't mean embracing your inner Pollyanna. What it does mean is that you let go of the victim role that you may have grown to see as normal. It was a role that Germaine seemed to play, even in the little things.

Ashley heard her frustrated coworker Germaine screaming in frustration, "Argh! I hate this thing!"

Ashley came out of her office to see what was wrong.

"It's this stupid pencil sharpener," Germaine said. "It breaks off the point every time. I hate it!"

"How long's it been like that?" asked Ashley.

"It's been like this for months!" Germaine said exasperated, playing her familiar victim role.

Ashley picked up the phone and paged the church secretary. "Hi, Amy. We have a broken pencil sharpener. Can you order us a new one?"

"Sure," said Amy. "Or you can just have the spare one I have in my closet. I'll bring it on over."

We're usually not as helpless as we think, but a victim mentality fogs our brain and makes us think there are no alternatives, even when there is often a solution waiting around the corner.

If your ministry is in a gloomy place, here's the good news: You get to decide how people feel about the youth ministry. You are the climate control system. Set the dial to "positive," and then keep your eye on the thermostat so no one turns it back.

FINDING RHYTHM

CHAPTER 43

For much of my life, the Sabbath had been a reminder of my failure as a Christian. I mean, really—does anyone honestly have time for that?

It's not likely that anyone in the church will ever compliment you for keeping this commandment. But there's a mighty good chance you'll get applauded for breaking it. I had always wanted a Sabbath, but I was just too busy to feel good about adding a full day off to my week.

I don't know about you, but I have rarely had a day when a ministry opportunity didn't come knocking on my door. And I made it a practice to try to answer every one. A full day of rest was a pipe dream— something only for people with less important things to do. So were evenings totally off. There were always a few more e-mails to be sent or lessons to be planned after dinner.

Over a decade ago, we invited Jim Burns to come do a little work with our youth staff—to help us see where we might be missing something, what parts of our program might need tweaking. For the first half of the day, Jim totally ignored our program. He just talked about us. He asked me a question, but before I answered, he asked my youth staff to predict how I might answer. Strangely, they all guessed correctly.

Jim asked, "If you could do anything in the world right now, if money and time were no object—dream your biggest dream—what would you do?"

My answer was telling, but not nearly as telling as the fact that it was so obvious to my staff. "My biggest dream right now," I said, "would be to take a nap. I just need to rest." Almost the exact answer my colleagues on staff gave about me.

I began to see Sabbath not as a chore or a discipline, but a solution. I began to shift from seeing Sabbath as an add-on luxury for people who had time on their hands to a crucial priority, a cornerstone of longevity in faith and ministry. I learned how to delight in a full day of resting in Christ and making a priority of enjoying my kids, my wife, and the windfall of being alive. It was a seismic shift, forcing the rest of the week to rearrange itself into six days of work rather than seven.

The crazy discovery was that I actually found myself getting *more* work done in six days than I previously had accomplished in seven. I began to experiment with the idea of *being* home when I was home (radical idea, I know) and leaving work at work. One of the secrets of loving your job in ministry for the long term is learning to live in God's rhythm of one day of intense withdrawal in every seven, a weekly rhythm that should include walking, sprinting, and resting.

In her book *Sacred Rhythms*, Ruth Haley Barton writes that God is already playing a song in our lives and that when we get ourselves in rhythm with that song, priorities and balance begin to fall into place naturally. If that all sounds a little fluffy to you, then consider the long, robust monastic tradition of having a "rule of life." A rule of life is not some sort of spiritual time management plan that we impose on top of what we're already doing. It involves punctuating and anchoring our days with a cadence of attending to God's presence in a way that brings order to the craziness of our lives.

Most youth workers I know can relate to Barton's description of "normal" in her introduction: "While I was trying harder and doing more, there was a yawning emptiness underneath it all that no amount of activity Christian or otherwise could fill." She calls it CFS: Christian Fatigue Syndrome.[8]

Adding layers of more and more spiritual stuff is not the answer. Neither is tweaking the tasks of our week. The only solution is to experience an internal shift in the way we order our lives, one week at a time.

I was surprised that for me, the rhythm is six days on and one day off, plus several evenings off each week, too. I work the same number of hours now, but it somehow feels like less because I'm fully working when I'm supposed to work and fully resting when I'm supposed to rest.

In the days before living with a weekly rhythm, I resented the fact that I would not have a full day off, so I would steal pockets of time—a Thursday afternoon movie or an extra-long lunch to go shopping. Now, I work each day straight through, knowing that a day of rest is just over the horizon.

In the evenings, a 30-minute project would loom ominously over my head for an entire evening as I tried to help with homework and put kids to bed. Neither my family nor my work got my full attention. What happened, I wondered, if any projects not finished before dinner had to be dealt with the next day? Dangling priorities began to be handled early in the next morning, freeing up my night to be truly present to the family God had given me to steward (or "husband").

One tool we love to use is one we call the rhythmic week calendar. It's a simple seven-column chart with three rows. The columns represent the seven days of the week, and the rows represent the three parts of the day: morning, afternoon, and evening. From those 21 slots, we start by designating a full day for Sabbath. Next we identify at least three more times to be home (or at least fully away from work). And then we build in a little something we call balcony time.

Balcony time is typically a full four-hour slot in the week, usually away from the office, when we touch none of the urgent things that are screaming for our attention. Instead, we stand in the "balcony" and look out over our entire ministry and life, determine priorities, make strategic shifts, and sketch out long-term plans. You can find tools to help you develop a rhythmic week at YMArchitects.com.

So if you want to love your work for the long haul, punctuate ever week with Sabbath withdrawal, and listen for that song that God is already singing over you and be courageous enough to dance to *that* rhythm.

GET USED TO THE MONEY

At nearly every staff meeting, Jacob made at least one cynical comment about his paycheck. He just couldn't stretch it enough to make ends meet. It was clear that he was feeling mistreated by the church, and he was sure the church needed to change.

He met with his pastor to request a raise. His pastor was sympathetic, but because of the recession and the drop in giving, it was all the church could do not to lay off staff, much less give raises. "But," his pastor asked, "how much more do you think you need a month?"

Jacob answered, "$200 would be amazing."

His boss said, "In ministry, it's just imperative that we remember that the paycheck from the church is not our provision. God is our provision, and God is fully capable of providing you an extra $200 a month apart from the church."

To Jacob, it sure seemed easy for his pastor, whose salary was much higher, to talk about God being our provision. He nodded but said nothing.

"I'm willing to take a risk with you," the pastor continued. "Let's look to God as your provision. If during the next year, you receive less than

$200 extra in any given month, I will personally write a check to you for the difference at the end of that month. In return, I want to ask a favor of you."

"What's that?" Jacob asked.

"I want you never to complain about money in our staff meetings again."

Jacob answered sheepishly, "You've got yourself a deal, sir."

The pastor never had to pay a dime.

Little extra jobs seemed to turn up each month without Jacob even looking. A generous family donated a washer and dryer. Month after month, the provision of at least $200 was always there.

But after that year, Jacob was still unhappy about his financial situation. It wasn't long before he admitted that he really wanted a different lifestyle for himself and his family. He quit his ministry job for a higher paying job outside of ministry that required fewer hours. And today, he continues to serve as an incredible, generous volunteer in his church.

I hope you hear us: There's nothing wrong with deciding you need a bigger paycheck. The mistake is blaming your church for not providing it for you. But before you quit your youth ministry job, let's get a little perspective.

A LITTLE PERSPECTIVE

According to a survey in the January/February 2010 edition of GROUP Magazine, the average full-time salary for a church employee with youth responsibilities was $35,000, not including benefits. That may not sound like a lot, but if there were a country made up of only youth pastors being paid an average youth-pastor salary, it would be one of the 20 wealthiest nations in the world.

Most people on this planet make a great deal less than we do, of course.[9] And the vast majority of them would consider it an enormous blessing to drive a 10-year-old Corolla and live in any one of our homes. If we're irritated, it's because we're only making 30 times as much as a citizen of Rwanda, and we wish it were closer to 40. That's a humbling perspective.

But you're right. We don't live in Rwanda. We live down the street from our wealthier friends and families who have cars with working air conditioners. We might be wealthy by world standards, but we make about 25 percent less than the average person in America.

Could it be, though, that there are perks to making enough but not a lot?

It certainly forces us to practice what we preach—that our provision is from God, not in a paycheck. Instead of living it up, we just might be forced to have to live it deep. Sure, a person can do both, but a youth pastor's paycheck has a way of forcing the issue.

Our friend Susan, a longtime youth minister with grown children, says that in hindsight, she appreciates what her tiny paycheck did in her own kids' lives. "They've learned how to prioritize the things that really matter," she says. She is thrilled by what she saw in her son's life as he has stepped into marriage. "They're not obsessed with going into debt to have all the latest stuff," she says. "It's just not part of their lifestyle."

Shane Claiborne wrote this in *The Irresistible Revolution*: "As I read Scriptures about how the first will be last, I started wondering why I was working so hard to be first."[10]

Perhaps the real gift of the smaller paycheck is that it nudges us toward living simply and trusting God to give all that we need. And we know a guy who might just be willing to bet you $200 a month to prove it.

HOW TO EAT YOUR BROCCOLI

—————— CHAPTER 45 ——————

Every job comes with its own fair share of tasks we don't want to do. That's why we get a paycheck. The places where you have fun all day, every day—those are called amusement parks, and we have to pay to get in.

Youth workers who love their ministries have figured out how to deal with the 20 to 30 percent of their jobs that they just don't enjoy. We call it "eating your broccoli."

A few friends have said, "That's a terrible analogy. I love to eat broccoli."

"Really," we ask. "Have you always been a fan, even when you were a kid?"

"Well, of course not," they say, "but I developed a taste for it, and now I eat it all the time."

Our point exactly.

We know that broccoli is good for us. It's a low-carb source of calcium, vitamin C, and antioxidants. I may not be crazy about the way it tastes or looks, but I need it (or something like it) if I'm going to live the kind of life I want to live.

There is a little broccoli in every job—things we would rather not do but things that, nevertheless, have a way of making our ministry immensely healthier in the long run. The broccoli of drafting a budget and a strong rationale for increases results in credibility and funding. Making phone calls to seven parents who say no leads to the eighth, who says yes to taking the burden of snack coordination off our back for a semester.

I don't know about you, but I have a natural appetite for Snickers® and Twinkies® (and checking my e-mail 10 times a day), but we can also develop a nuanced appreciation of what's good for us (planning, recruiting, or moving beyond our comfort zone).

BROCCOLI-PORTION-CONTROL STRATEGIES

The great news is that you don't have to do all the broccoli work yourself. There's a good chance you've got someone in your church who likes every kind of broccoli that you hate. Someone finds satisfaction in keeping the kitchen clean or in running a $5,000 fundraiser. Share that piece of broccoli with someone who loves it.

It might be time to try different recipes and find ways to cook your broccoli a little differently. Here are a few recipes:

- Stuffing envelopes by yourself isn't what you signed up for, but you can turn it into great bonding time with students you've been wanting to connect with.

- Asking unfamiliar students to just sit around a table and talk might feel like torture, but a dinner and movie night with a group of guys you've been trying to connect with might actually work out.

Complaining, of course, never makes a distasteful task disappear, but trading can. Think about how you can trade duties with someone else on your team. ("I'll take care of calling the students this week, which I love, if you'll clean and decorate the youth room, which you love.")

Once you have the broccoli portion down to the smallest serving possible, don't let it sit there and get mushy. Eat it right away.

I'm not naturally a big veggie fan. I've discovered, though, that if I wait to eat my broccoli until the end of the meal, I like it even less; the bitter broccoli juice runs all over my plate. It seeps into the food I love and has a way of spoiling the taste. And if I wait until the end of the meal, there's a good chance I'll be so full that I'll avoid the green stuff altogether.

When it comes to necessary but unwanted tasks, procrastination is not your friend. When you put off your least favorite, high-priority work until the end of the week, the negativity you feel about those tasks has a way of seeping into everything you do all week long, spoiling even the parts of your ministry that you love. Go ahead: Get your least favorite, gotta-do task out of the way, and then enjoy the rest of your day.

And who knows, once you stop avoiding it, you might find yourself actually developing a taste for broccoli.

KNOWING WHEN
TO LEAVE

CHAPTER 46

After three months of detailed accountability for work he was consistently not getting done, Tim was tired. He was tired of the micro-managing, tired of the expectation that he do things that he didn't really want to do, tired of not really wanting to come to work anymore. He told his supervisor, "This job is not fun anymore. Sometimes I feel like throwing in the towel and moving back to Indiana."

Tim's associate pastor supervisor was quiet for a long minute. She tilted her head and said, "That would not entirely disappoint me."

The next day when we met with Tim, he asked, "What was that supposed to mean?"

It meant that Tim wasn't great at picking up on the clues his church was handing him. Because church people are famously non-confrontational, we sometimes have to read between the lines.

But your departure (which will come for every youth worker eventually) need not be conflicted or acrimonious. Sometimes the change will come as the church's decision. Sometimes it's the youth pastor's decision. Sometimes it's mutual. Other times it's just a bad fit. Whatever the reason—frustration, fit, finances, or something else—it's in your interest to make the decision yourself instead of having it made for you.

It's a little bit like the advice we have been known to give a "stuck" dating couple: If you find yourself spending more energy bickering *about* your relationship than actually living it, perhaps it's time to consider a change.

BUT WHAT ABOUT LONGEVITY?

A friend of mine recently quoted the late Bart Giamatti, who served as president of Yale University and commissioner of Major League Baseball, who said something I found fascinating:

"Never stay in a job more than eight years. Otherwise, you'll be dealing almost entirely with problems you've made."[11]

Though spoken as a joke at the end of his eight-year tenure at Yale, his words started me wondering: Is there a point at which we can stay *too long* in a particular youth ministry position?

Coming up on my 25th year at my church, I ask this question with more than a passing interest. The truth is that all the challenges I currently face in ministry are *mine*—either ones I created or one I couldn't overcome.

We've been fanatics for long-term youth ministry for a long time. And we both love the transformation that came in our groups after hanging around for six years, long enough to be the youth pastors for every teenager in our programs.

But over a few years of coaching churches, we have seen a few youth workers who just might have overstayed their effectiveness. So just in case you happen to be one of those, we've created a little "I Know I've Stayed Too Long If…" survey (check all that apply):

I KNOW I'VE STAYED TOO LONG IF...

- ☐ I haven't learned anything new about youth ministry in the last five years

- ☐ I can't talk about my senior pastor (or the parents or that nemesis elder) without inwardly rolling my eyes

- [ ] I don't take any input from volunteers seriously until they have been with me for five years

- [ ] The last new idea I tried came from one of the Ideas books

- [ ] I have great volunteer leaders, but they're getting tired, and the younger people in our church just aren't committed

- [ ] If I am honest, I stopped liking teenagers years ago

- [ ] I am secretly excited when someone else's new idea fails (like I thought it would)

- [ ] I am jealous when students build closer relationships with my volunteers than with me

If you checked more than half these statements, it's time to consider the possibility that your longevity may not be doing anyone any favors. Experience in youth ministry is a gift from God, but experience makes some people bitter and stale—bitter at the church for suggesting we might need to think differently and grow, stale by an obsessive focus on getting our jobs done as easily as possible.

But if you can keep your heart in the game, if you can joyfully accept fresh input (especially when it feels like criticism), and if you can continue to love your church in all its brokenness, please stay.

A FINAL WORD

Hey, you didn't flip to the back of the book and read the last chapter first, did you?

We know people like that. They start with the final chapter to see how the story ends. That helps them decide whether they want to read the rest of the book. It takes away a lot of the dramatic tension, but some people like it better that way.

If that's what you're looking for, here it is.

The end of the story—our story, our students' stories, our ministries' stories—goes like this: God wins.

Maybe that steals away some of the drama for you. We hope so. We could all do with a little less drama.

God wins. No matter what you're facing in youth ministry right now— whether you're hoping to get hired or whether you've been at the same church for 20 years—God wins.

DELEGATE UP

We can name any student in our ministry and say, "That one belongs to you, God." When we've been rejected for the third time by a teenager who continues to make foolish decisions, we find an anchor in remembering that God cares more than we do. When a student has decided to hide from us, we can at least take comfort in knowing that nothing can separate him or her from the love of Christ.

Sometimes we can sense the Spirit of God saying, "I'll take it from here," and we delegate up. At other times, God seems happy to delegate things right back to us. Either way, we're not alone.

CRISIS IS INEVITABLE; FREAK-OUT IS OPTIONAL

As you step into the next chapter of your ministry, we hope you'll claim two promises from Jesus found in John 16:33.

1. *"In this world you will have trouble."*

2. *"I have overcome the world."*

If you've been in youth ministry for more than three weeks, you've experienced the first promise. When you work with teenagers, crazy things happen. Some are little adventures. Some are heartbreaking. We deal with the loss of innocence and the loss of life; with drugs, depression, and dropouts; with complaining coworkers and parents on the warpath.

All of that is right on schedule. Jesus promised it, remember? But redemption, compassion, and miraculous do-overs are part of the story, too. In the middle of crises bigger than we can handle alone, we can be sure of what we hope for and certain of what we can't yet see (Hebrews 11:1). Some days (OK, every day), we need to remind ourselves that Jesus really has overcome the world.

BEYOND PEACE

It was the Friday night before Jeff's first retreat, and he was sure it was going to be a mess. He finally went to bed at 1 a.m. but was up five minutes later, remembering he'd forgotten to pack the cooler. He found it in the garage, set it out for the next day, and crawled back into bed. He was up again five minutes later, this time to print out directions to the retreat center for all the drivers.

In the fifth middle-of-the-night rising from bed, an idea came into his head—something about anxiety being overcome by peace beyond understanding (Philippians 4:6-7). He grabbed a random piece of paper and with a fat felt-tip marker wrote these words: "Jeff, is God in a panic over this?"

He propped the sign on the nightstand next to his bed—and slept soundly.

We can only finish this long race if we remember our place on the team: The teenagers that we love already have a Savior. And we are not it. The job of ministry feels too big because it is. It is a God-sized job. When we remember that, we succeed.

Archbishop Oscar Romero served the people of El Salvador and was assassinated in 1980 while leading worship in San Salvador. We can think of no better blessing to leave you than these wise words on ministry that have surrounded the legacy of one who died living them:

> It helps, now and then, to step back and take a long view.
> The kingdom is not only beyond our efforts,
> it is even beyond our vision.
> We accomplish in our lifetime only a tiny fraction
> of the magnificent enterprise that is God's work.
> Nothing we do is complete, which is a way of saying
> that the kingdom always lies beyond us.
>
> No statement says all that could be said.
> No prayer fully expresses our faith.
> No confession brings perfection.
> No pastoral visit brings wholeness.
> No program accomplishes the church's mission.
> No set of goals and objectives includes everything.
>
> This is what we are about.
> We plant the seeds that one day will grow.
> We water seeds already planted, knowing that they hold future promise.
> We lay foundations that will need further development.
> We provide yeast that produces far beyond our capabilities.
> We cannot do everything, and there is a sense of liberation in realizing that.

This enables us to do something, and to do it very well.
It may be incomplete,
but it is a beginning, a step along the way,
an opportunity for the Lord's grace to enter and do the rest.

We may never see the end results,
but that is the difference
between the master builder and the worker.
We are workers, not master builders; ministers, not messiahs.
We are prophets of a future not our own.

Amen.[12]

ENDNOTES

1. Edwin Friedman, *A Failure of Nerve* (New York, NY: Seabury Books, 2007).

2. Mike Nappa, *What I Wish My Youth Leader Knew About Youth Ministry* (Cincinnati, OH: Standard Publishing Company, 1999).

3. Christopher Hibbert, *Disraeli: A Personal History* (New York, NY: HarperCollins Publishers, 2004).

4. Malcolm Gladwell, *Outliers: The Story of Success* (New York, NY: Little, Brown and Company, 2008).

5. Jim Collins, *Good to Great and the Social Sectors: A Monograph to Accompany Good to Great* (New York, NY: HarperCollins Publishers, 2005).

6. Doug Fields, *Purpose Driven Youth Ministry* (Grand Rapids, MI: Zondervan, 1998).

7. Malcolm Gladwell, *Blink: The Power of Thinking Without Thinking* (New York, NY: Little, Brown and Company, 2005).

8. Ruth Haley Barton, *Sacred Rhythms* (Westmont, IL: InterVarsity Press, 2006).

9. The standard of living figures come from the World Bank statistics that equal out the numbers to account for cost of living and exchange rates. http://data.worldbank.org/country

10. Shane Claiborne, *The Irresistible Revolution: Living as an Ordinary Radical* (Grand Rapids, MI: Zondervan, 2006).

11. http://archive.youthministry.com/details.asp?ID=7157

12. According to the March 28, 2004, edition of the National Catholic Reporter: These words have come to be known as "The Romero Prayer" and have come to represent the profound legacy of his ministry. It is now clear that they were originally written not by Romero but by Ken Untener.

A PERSONAL
SEARCH TIMELINE

Wait a second.

Before you get started, we're assuming you've had a few honest discussions with yourself, your spouse, and God before you leap into this search process. We're assuming that you are working with youth now as a volunteer or staff person and that your eyes are wide-open about yourself and youth ministry—warts and all. If not, check out the first five chapters before you go any further.

But if you're ready to launch into an abnormal search for your dream job in youth ministry, here's a quick checklist. We've even included a very rough timeline. Feel free to speed it up, but we can't think of anything you'll want to leave out. This search process involves some hard work, and parts of it are just plain boring, but it offers a time-proven, successful strategy that moves you beyond simply wishing and hoping—the strategy most other candidates are using.

Are you ready to be intentional about your search? Then let's get going.

☐ Day 1—Determine the parameters of your search. You may have geographical or financial limitations that will narrow the scope of your search. For example, if you need to stay in your current state or make a certain salary level, that factor will quite naturally limit your options.

☐ Day 2—Develop your pool of possible contacts. You'll want to start with 100 or so, remembering that your acquaintances may be more help to you than your friends, since your friends tend to know the same people you do.

Develop a tracking chart for your 100 contacts (see Appendix B) to help you keep up with when you want to follow up with each contact. The tracking chart should include e-mail addresses, phone numbers, an explanation of the connection, a section for notes from your contacts, and a follow-up date.

☐ Day 3—Get your résumé drafted and, if possible, show it to three or four senior pastors, asking for feedback about anything they would recommend you change.

Make phone appointments with your potential references. Ask for a quick 15 minutes to go through a few questions like the ones in the "Reference Please," Chapter 10.

☐ Days 5-10—Make a personal connection with at least 50 of your 100 contacts via e-mail, phone call, or personal message on Facebook. Though this is not a group e-mail, you can use the same basic information, with a personal introduction that reminds the reader of your connection to them (such as, "My pastor, Jim Smith, suggested I contact you..."). In these contacts, you are not just looking for people who might be hiring; you are looking for people who might know someone who might be hiring. Ask the question, "Is there anyone else you would recommend that I talk to as I search?"

- Day 6—Post a brief announcement on Facebook® about the kind of job you are feeling called to, and invite your friends to recommend people you might want to connect with. First comb through your profile, pages, and galleries to clean up anything that would embarrass you in front of a search committee.

- Day 7—Begin looking at positions that have been posted on the Internet. You can type "Youth Ministry Job Boards" into a search engine and find several good ones. We sponsor two websites that also offer that service: YMArchitects.com and HireAYouthPastor.com.

- Days 11-17—Connect with the rest of your 100+ contacts.

- Day 20—Contact denominational or association representatives in appropriate parts of the country. Your pastor might have some suggestions, and most can be found on the Internet with a search engine. If you are doing a national search, start by focusing on your top 10 target locations.

- Day 21—Determine a follow-up date for *each* of your 100+ contacts. Generally, it's two weeks after your most recent communication with them.

- Day 22—Tap into existing networks of youth pastors. Start with the National Network of Youth Ministry (nnym.com). From there, you can use a search engine to hunt for phrases like "Youth Ministry Network" and the cities you're interested in.

THE FOLLOWING MONTHS: FAITHFUL REPETITION

- **Every day**

  - Return all phone calls within 24 hours of receiving them— even if it's just a short "Thanks for your e-mail; I look forward to…"

  - Return all e-mails within 48 hours.

- **Every week**

  - Use your tracking list to pinpoint any contacts who have not responded in two weeks or more. Send a follow-up e-mail "in case the first one didn't reach you." Include some new piece of information about yourself.

- Check back with your top churches that have not responded in the past two or three weeks. It's OK to ask about their time schedule for the process.

  - Ask, "Is there any more information I can supply you?"

  - Comment on something you might have seen in their church newsletter or website.

  - Send a link to a photo gallery from your latest youth event. (They can always ignore it.)

- One out of 10 churches will be annoyed by your follow-up, but most will appreciate your diligence. Be prepared to receive no response or a short "still in committee" e-mail. Search committees aren't always speedy or efficient.

- Add another 10-20 contacts to your list weekly and make a connection.

  - Each time a person e-mails to say they don't know of any openings, reply with a short "Thanks; do you know of someone else I should contact during my search?"

  - Use the Internet to explore additional regional representatives of denominations and associations.

If there's a position or two that you are very interested in, it's OK to let those churches know when you have started the interview process with another church.

THREE-MONTH CHECKUP

If after three months of working this process, you are disappointed in the number of churches who are interested in you, find an honest friend who understands youth ministry to help you review your résumé, your cover letter, and even your fit for youth ministry. After making any necessary tweaks, begin the process again.

AFTER YOU ARE HIRED

Don't stop sending out résumés and interviewing until you have written confirmation of being hired. You want to be sure you have a deal before you announce it to your mom and everyone else.

Then contact any churches that said they were considering you. Thank them and let them know you've been hired.

And thank God! You're hired!

SAMPLE TRACKING
LIST FOR CONTACTS

Name	E-mail	Phone	First Contact	Most Recent Contact	Next Contact	Connection	Notes

ACKNOWLEDGEMENTS

None of us is as smart as all of us.

- Ken Blanchard

This book is, in many ways, an anthology of other people's stories, wisdom, and experiences. We're grateful for the privilege of being observers and partners with so many friends in youth ministry and specifically for the dozens of youth ministry rookies and veterans whose stories have found their way into these pages, particularly those of Duffy Robbins, Ryan Wallace, Jim Burns, and Steve Schneeberger.

We want to thank first the youth and adult leaders of First Presbyterian Church in Nashville, Tennessee, and Christ United Methodist Church in Venice, Florida. The roller coaster ride of life together, the breath-stealing belly laughs, the unashamed sweat, and times the tears have flowed freely are a sweet reminder that someone greater than us is in charge—because we clearly are not.

The unique giftedness and passion of the youth staffs at First Presbyterian (Katy, Scott, Courtney, Teddy, Trey, Linda, Ryan, Ellie, and Erika) and Christ United Methodist (Susan, Marcia, Deanna, Sean, and Bekah) have shaped not only much of what is written in these pages but also who we are as well. Thanks for walking boldly into ambiguity every day.

We are grateful for that curious cohort of holy friends on our Youth Ministry Architects lead team (Betsy, Colyer, Dave, David, Jen, Lesleigh, Lynn, Sara, Stephanie), who have contributed to many of these ideas, tested others, and constantly find ways to make us better.

Our growing family of YMA churches has entrusted us with the awesome privilege of mentoring, befriending, and partnering in this mission to build sustainable youth ministries one church at a time. It was in your churches that so many ideas in this book were discovered and moved from vague theories to time-tested practices. We are grateful.

Thanks to our already busy friends who took time to read and improve these pages before they saw the light of day: Jules Postema, Andrew Suite, David Dunn-Rankin, Ben Kane, Jeff Wertz, Ann Bailey, Caroline Rossini, Becky Ellenberger, and to our partners at Group and Simply Youth Ministry—Rick Lawrence, Doug Fields, Scott Firestone, Andy Brazelton, and Nadim Najm.

And now for a few personal words...

I (Mark) am particularly grateful for

- Jeff, for partnering with me in YMA's incremental revolution and for laughing louder than anyone else when I try to be funny

- My pastor, Todd Jones, and the elders and staff of First Presbyterian Church, who grant me much more freedom and honor than I deserve

- Chan Sheppard, my running buddy and treasured friend

- The pioneers at the Center for Youth Ministry Training—Deech, Lesleigh, Andrew, and Mindi—who are asking all the right questions about the training of indispensable youth pastors

- Adam, Sara, Debbie, Trey, and Leigh, who have long since moved from being our children to being our dearest friends and partners in the gospel

- My bride, Susan; you give me an unfair advantage.

I (Jeff) am especially grateful for my family, colleagues and coaches:

- Mark, no one could ask for a better trailblazer, leader and friend. Thanks for inviting me along.

- My pastor, Jerry, and people of Christ United Methodist for loving God and loving kids—and loving them in the right order. Thanks for taking a leap of faith for me long ago and continuing to bless my life.

- Fellow workers in the field: Larry, Al, Bob, Bobby, Cheryl, Dan, Dick, Edna Kate, Esther, Glenn, Jack, JoEllen, Ken, Kevin, Kyla,

Lenee, Linda, Michele, Paul, Sandra, and my buddies at One Christ/Won City.

- The bosses who gave me room to fail forward and learn: Dad, Steve, Jim, Mark, Bob, Marsha, Dave, Buddy, and the guy at Milton's Pizza.

- My kind and wise family: Dad, Mom, Peter, David, Debbie, and Mike, whose insights are woven throughout these pages.

- Matthew and Katie—you are exactly what we dreamed of.

- Mary Lou—you are more.

And to the God who is the only indispensable one—who grants us both humility and value by allowing us to be minor characters in a major story.

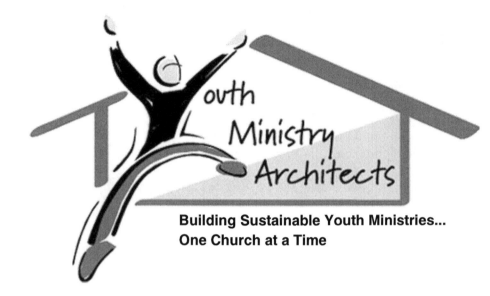

Building Sustainable Youth Ministries...
One Church at a Time

THE PARABLE OF THE HOLEY MAN

A man falls into a deep hole and finds himself stuck—alone and in the dark. For a few anxious hours, he tries to jump or climb his way out, but the 20-foot walls are slippery and cold. It doesn't take long before he gives up and collapses in a dark corner.

Just when he thinks there's no way out, an old friend walks by the hole and peers over to see his buddy.

"Hey," he says, "I see you fell into a hole."

"Yes, I did," says the man. "I feel so helpless."

"Of course you do," says the friend at the top of the well. "You should be more careful. Even I could have told you this is what happens when you don't watch where you're going." He chuckles, then pauses for a moment. "Hey, just kidding buddy," he says. "I feel your pain. Listen, I'll be sure to pray for you. Stay warm." And he walks away.

A few tense hours later, another friend walks by. "Hey," she says, "I see you fell into a hole."

"Yes," says the man. "Can you help me?"

"Of course I can," says the friend. "I fell into a hole once. In fact I have this great book about how to avoid holes in the future. Here—catch!" She tosses the book into the deep, dark hole. And she walks away.

Just about the time the man has abandoned all hope, a third friend comes by. "Hey," he says, ""I see you fell into a hole."

"Yes," says the man. "I don't think I'll ever get out." "Scoot over," says the third friend, and he climbs down into the hole. "Are you crazy?" says the man. "Now we're both stuck down here!" "Don't panic," says his friend, "I've been in this hole before, and I know the way out."

At Youth Ministry Architects, we want to be that third friend. Established in 2002 with a vision of building sustainable youth ministries, one church at a time, we are the veteran youth and children's workers who have been "in the holes" of youth ministry more times than we can count. But we know the way out. YMA is the nation's leader in youth ministry consulting, and we partner with churches, clergy, youth ministers, and volunteers who want to move beyond the common challenges that create stuckness and less than stellar results in youth and children's ministry.

We have coached about 200 churches in over 15 denominations to establish personalized strategic plans for building thriving, sustainable ministries that have a deep impact on young lives. Like custom architects, we have no interest in imposing a one-size-fits-all model. We start by listening and together develop a blueprint for moving ministries from where they are now to where their stakeholders feel God is calling them to be. And then we walk alongside them to ensure the renovation takes place in a sustainable way.

To learn more, read *Sustainable Youth Ministry* by Mark DeVries, visit YMArchitects.com, or contact us at info@ymarchitects.com or 877-462-5718.